The Welfare State in the European Union

Economic and Social Perspectives

The Welfare State in the European Union

Economic and Social Perspectives

Pierre Pestieau

OXFORD
UNIVERSITY PRESS

OXFORD

UNIVERSITY PRESS

Great Clarendon Street, Oxford OX2 6DP

Oxford University Press is a department of the University of Oxford.
It furthers the University's objective of excellence in research, scholarship,
and education by publishing worldwide in

Oxford New York

Auckland Cape Town Dar es Salaam Hong Kong Karachi
Kuala Lumpur Madrid Melbourne Mexico City Nairobi
New Delhi Shanghai Taipei Toronto

With offices in

Argentina Austria Brazil Chile Czech Republic France Greece
Guatemala Hungary Italy Japan Poland Portugal Singapore
South Korea Switzerland Thailand Turkey Ukraine Vietnam

Oxford is a registered trade mark of Oxford University Press
in the UK and in certain other countries

Published in the United States
by Oxford University Press Inc., New York

© P. Pestieau, 2006

British Library Cataloguing in Publication Data

Data available

Library of Congress Cataloging in Publication Data

Data available

Typeset by Newgen Imaging Systems (P) Ltd., Chennai, India
Printed in Great Britain
on acid-free paper by
Biddles Ltd., King's Lynn, Norfolk

ISBN 0–19–926101–6   978–0–19–926101–7
ISBN 0–19–926102–4 (Pbk.)   978–0–19–926102–4 (Pbk.)

1 3 5 7 9 10 8 6 4 2

☐ CONTENTS

☐ PREFACE

The origin of this book goes back to the deep uneasiness I have felt since very early in my life as an economist. Increasingly squeezed between two contrasting views on social policy, I have experienced what the French call two 'pensées uniques.' According to the first view, market forces should be given priority over any considerations, be they social, cultural or political. On the other hand, the second view holds that objectives of equity and social cohesion have precedence over those of economic efficiency and growth. Given my training and my work in public economics, particularly in second-best social optimization, I find myself at odds with these two polar views. I suggest an intermediate and more balanced approach, one that simultaneously takes into account efficiency as well as equity considerations.

My vision of the welfare state, as expanded in this book, is the product of many contributions to my development. Many people have shared with me their aspiration for a world in which efficiency is pursued with constant concern for equity, and in which redistribution and poverty alleviation are achieved within a setting of allocative efficiency and economic growth. I am indebted to my teachers, Jacques Drèze and Joseph Stiglitz, who have infused in me their enthusiasm and insight to pursue a rigorous analysis of public sector economics. Likewise, I am grateful to a number of co-authors and friends with whom I have worked on the topics and ideas presented in this book: Maurice Marchand and Philippe Michel (both of whom have left us too early), Robin Boadway, Helmuth Cremer, Denis Kessler, André Masson, Sergio Perelman, Uri Possen.

I would also like to mention younger colleagues with whom I have worked over the years, and who have offered me a different point of view, that of another generation, with respect to the issues discussed here: Motohiro Sato, Jean-Marie Lozachmeur, Georges Casamatta, Alain Jousten, Luc Arrondel, Jean-Pierre Vidal, Maria del Mar Racionero and Manuel Leite Monteiro. I have also benefited from visits to research centers that provided the environment ideal for big pushes in the progress of this book: the CES in Munich, the Mario Einaudi Center at Cornell University and the Research Department at the World Bank.

My thanks also go to Claudine Chmielewski, who provided expert secretarial support throughout the years, to Marianne David, who edited my typescript and improved its readability with dedication and talent, and to Mathieu Lefèbvre, who updated the statistical evidence up to the last minute.

Finally, I dedicate this book to my two children, Sophie and Daniel, trusting that they share my concern for justice and fairness.

1 Introduction

KEY CONCEPTS

Altruism

constitutional approach

efficiency or Pareto efficiency

equity

equity–efficiency trade-off

leaky bucket

market failure

merit good

political economy

veil of ignorance

1.1 Questioning the welfare state

Unquestionably, the welfare state is a fundamental and distinguishing feature of the European social model. A major achievement of post-war Europe, it has enabled societies to cope with tremendous economic and social upheavals and adaptations. Social cohesion, which is the basis and the outcome of the welfare state, is an objective of European Union member states as much now as it was in 1945, when the welfare state began. Yet, in recent years the welfare state has come under increasing attack. Although in Europe there continues to be a large degree of consensus that it is the responsibility of government to insure that nobody who is poor, sick, disabled, unemployed and old is left deprived, there are mounting calls to roll back spending on the welfare state. Two main charges are raised: that it fails to achieve some of its main objectives, and that it is responsible for a decline in economic performance.

Although we believe that these charges are to be taken seriously, one needs to remember past achievements to know how much we would lose were the welfare state to disappear. We believe that saving the welfare state is a top priority, one that is as important as saving the Parthenon or the Mona Lisa.

In this book we intend to provide a balanced and informed account of the current functioning and performance of the welfare state in the European Union,[1] as well as some thoughts regarding its prospects in an increasingly integrated world. Written by an economist whose concern is both equity and

---

[1] Throughout the book we deal with the European Union before 5.1.04; that is a community of 15 and not 25 members. This will be denoted EU15 or even EU12 for the European Community with 12 members.

efficiency, this book gives a set of answers to a number of important questions regarding the current social situation of the European Union. These questions concern the actual working and expected evolution of its welfare states, and are the subject of academic research among economists, political scientists, sociologists. More importantly, they are the daily concern of European policymakers and citizens.

The following questions correspond to 14 chapters here contained:

1. What is the welfare state? What are its functions? How can it be distinguished from concepts such as social protection and social insurance?

2. What is the current state of poverty, deprivation and social inequality in the European Union? Can we say that the welfare state contributes to their reduction? What can be expected in the near future?

3. What is the size and the structure of the welfare state? Does it vary across countries, over time? Can we, in particular, speak of a decline in social spending in the recent past?

4. How is the welfare state financed in different countries? Does it rely on payroll taxes or on general taxation?

5. What types of social protection exist in Europe? More precisely, are benefits linked to contributions, attached to means testing or are they universalist?

6. One often hears that factor mobility and economic integration make it difficult to redistribute income, thus leading to what is called social dumping. How serious is such a threat?

7. Is the welfare state a real obstacle to economic efficiency and economic growth because of distorted incentives and large deficits?

8. Can we say that, compared to market activities, the welfare state's activities are costly and inefficient? What is the performance of the welfare state with regard to fighting poverty and reducing inequalities?

9. What are the comparative advantages of social and private insurance in reducing uncertainty for the individual?

10. Social security in Europe is mainly unfunded and publicly managed. How can it meet the challenge of demographic ageing and economic stagnation?

11. Health care in Europe is public, and it faces huge financial problems. How can one maintain its financial soundness and universal accessibility?

12. Can we really assert that there is an unavoidable trade-off between poverty and unemployment, and that most European countries, except the UK and Ireland, have chosen the latter?

13. Most European countries have programs of family allowances that pursue certain objectives: foster fertility, avoid child poverty and achieve horizontal equity. What is the performance of the welfare state regarding these objectives?

14. Finally, how seriously can we consider privatization as a partial way of solving some of the problems of the European welfare state? More generally, should the welfare state in Europe be saved at all costs? If so, how?

To preview the answer to the last question, it is our conviction that the welfare state must be saved, and quickly. Its main functions cannot be fulfilled by either the market or the family. The fulfillment of those functions is an essential part of what can be considered a modern and democratic society. Reforming it is of utmost urgency because its present operation cannot resist the challenges that lie ahead. Saving the welfare state is possible, but it requires some fundamental changes in the institutions. Above all, it requires changes in the behavior of European citizens who all too often, as the saying goes, 'want to have their cake and eat it too.'

Over the last decades, demographic, economic and social changes have occurred across the European Union with profound implications for the welfare states. The ageing of the population, the decreasing employment rate, the change in the gender balance, the increase in the demand for support services are typical of these changes. Yet most important is the phenomenon of vanishing compliance and the increasing opportunism of all the economic players. We are talking about ageing but healthy workers who use disability insurance to get a well-paid early retirement. We are talking about employers who use the unemployment insurance to get rid of workers they find too costly; or farmers who insist on keeping subsidies that no longer have any economic justification. We are talking about the practise on the part of the national governments of tax competition and social dumping to attract foreign investors and employment. Changing such opportunistic behavior and rediscovering some sense of solidarity are surely big challenges facing our welfare states.

The rest of this introduction is devoted to the definition of the concepts of welfare state, social protection and social insurance, and to their rationale, as well as to the trade-off between equity and efficiency.

1.2 **Definitions and objectives**

It is tempting not to define the welfare state. As Barr (1992)[2] puts it, 'defining the welfare state continues to baffle writers and much high-grade effort has

---

[2] Compared to Barr (1998), this book focuses more on the redistribution issue and less on the insurance mission of the welfare state.

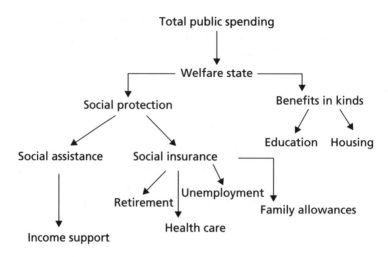

Figure 1.1. Welfare state and social protection

been vested in the search.'[3] Indeed, let us just indicate what it comprises and what its functions are. The welfare state consists of a number of programs through which the government pursues the goal of social protection on behalf of citizens against certain categories of risk, of social assistance for the needy, and of encouraging the consumption of certain services such as education, housing and child care. This is depicted in Figure 1.1.

These programs were introduced to meet certain objectives, the two most important being to relieve poverty and to provide a sense of security to all. When assessing the performance of the welfare state, it is important to do so with respect to these goals. Assistance and insurance are not the only objectives of the welfare state. Some of its programs also have effects on macroeconomic stabilization and growth. Conversely, some assistance and some insurance can be achieved by institutions other than the government. Insurance can be provided by the market, and both insurance and assistance can be provided by the family and more broadly by the non-profit sector. As will be shown, neither the market nor the family can have the negative impact on the working of the economy that is attributed to the welfare state. Yet, the scope of the family and that of the non-profit sector are much narrower than that of the welfare state; further, the market achieves little, if any, redistribution.

[3] One could use Sandmo's (1995) definition: 'The welfare state is a subsection of the public sector, concerned with redistribution (via social security and social assistance) and the provision of those social goods which have a strong redistributive element, like health care and education.' See also Sandmo (1991).

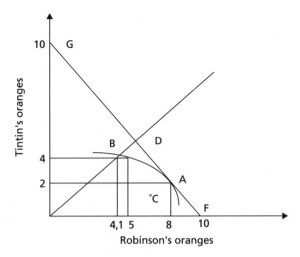

Figure 1.2. Equity and efficiency

1.3 **Equity versus efficiency**

Throughout this book, we shall be concerned with the quandary equity–efficiency that is at the heart of modern public economics. To illustrate this quandary, consider a simple economy with two individuals, whom we shall refer to as Robinson Crusoe and Tintin. Assume initially that Robinson Crusoe has eight oranges, while Tintin has only two. This seems inequitable. Assume that we play the role of government and attempt to transfer three oranges from Robinson Crusoe to Tintin, but in the process one orange gets lost. This refers to Okun's (1974) notion that money transferred from rich to poor is carried in a *leaky bucket*: 'The money must be carried from the rich to the poor in a leaky bucket. Some of it will simply disappear in transit, so the poor will not receive all the money that is taken from the rich.' Hence Robinson Crusoe ends up with five oranges, and Tintin with four. We have eliminated most of the inequity, but the total number of oranges available has been diminished. Thus we see a trade-off between efficiency, the total number of oranges available, and equity, the way they are divided.

This trade-off between equity and efficiency is at the heart of many discussions of public policy. It is often represented as in Figure 1.2 by the AB curve. A is the initial endowment, B is the equal-sharing allocation which involves a loss of more than one orange.

To get more equity some amount of efficiency must be sacrificed. Two questions are debated. First, there is disagreement about the nature of the trade-off. In order to reduce inequality, how much efficiency do we have to give up? Will one or two oranges be lost in the process of transferring three oranges from

Robinson to Tintin? For instance, the attempt to reduce inequality by progressive taxation is commonly regarded as giving rise to work disincentives, thereby reducing efficiency. How big are these disincentives? This is the question to which we will return.

Secondly, there is disagreement on how much value should be assigned to a decrease in inequality, and how much to a decrease in efficiency. Some people claim that inequality is the central problem of society, and that society should simply minimize the extent of inequality, regardless of the efficiency consequences. Others claim that efficiency is the central issue. Still others maintain that in the long run the best way to help the poor is not to worry about how the pie is to be divided, but rather to 'increase' the size of the pie, by growing as rapidly as possible so that there is more for everyone.

Maximizing efficiency is frequently equated with maximizing the value of national income. A program is said to introduce an inefficiency if it reduces national income, for example, through discouraging work or investment. By contrast, a program is said to promote equality if it transfers resources from someone richer to someone poorer.

Although this would provide a first approximation, economists have devoted considerable attention to assessing the circumstances in which using such measures might be misleading or inapplicable. Suppose the government increased taxes and squandered the proceeds, while, in order to maintain the same standard of living, individuals worked harder and longer than they had previously. National income as conventionally measured would go up, but 'efficiency'—as we normally think of it—would decrease.

To assess efficiency gains, one uses the concept of Pareto improvement instead of national income. To characterize an efficient allocation, one speaks of Pareto optimality or efficiency. In Figure 1.2, going from C to A we see a Pareto improving move such that everyone is better off (or at least not worse off). Both A and D are Pareto optimal, since from these points one cannot make someone better off without making someone else worse off.

If one had to choose the most important proposition in modern economic theory, one would very likely pick Adam Smith's 'invisible hand': a *laissez-faire* economy resulting in a Pareto-efficient allocation. In other words, the competitive market leads to a point on the line FG in Figure 1.2. The allocations F, A, D, G are all Pareto-optimal, which does not mean that from an equity viewpoint they are equally desirable. Thus even if the market is Pareto-optimal, there are grounds for government action if the resulting distribution of income, or consumption, is socially undesirable or even repugnant.

There are other reasons for government activity and these are the so-called market failures. Imperfect competition, externalities, public goods, imperfect information are sources of such failures. To illustrate: the market outcome can be an allocation such as C in Figure 1.2.

Note, however, that the presence of market failures is not a sufficient condition for government intervention. One has to make sure that the correction itself is not going to cost more than the slack it intends to correct. Indeed, we have seen that redistribution implies some efficiency cost. This is also true of other programs, even those aimed at restoring efficiency. Modern public economics is very much concerned with the right balance between market and state failures. It is noteworthy that from 1945 to about 1980, the pendulum first swung towards market failures; most recently, over the last two decades, it has swung towards state failures. Now it seems to be swinging back towards market failures.

1.4 Why the welfare state?

There are a number of theories that explain the birth and the development of the welfare state. Such explanation is, indeed, needed when starting from a market or a *laissez-faire* economy that leads to an efficient outcome at best, but does not have any prior concern for equity.

Without being exhaustive, we suggest several explanations for this: market failures, social contract, ethical norms, paternalistic altruism, class interest, political economy. These different explanations can be combined as we will show throughout this book.

1. Market failure. As just seen, there are several areas where the market forces are not able to achieve efficiency. When individual decisions have a positive, or a negative, effect on the welfare or the behavior of other agents, the price system is often unable to reflect what is called an 'externality.' For example, if investing in education has a benefit not only for me, but also for society as a whole, my market choice will be guided exclusively by my individual return, and not by the social benefit it implies. Here is a clear case for public intervention in the name of efficiency.

2. Behind the *veil of ignorance* social contract. One can imagine that in adopting a given welfare state, people are guided by some degree of impersonality. They are in a situation such that they don't know their ability, their health status, their life-expectancy just as if they were at time 0 of their own existence and that of their offspring. Behind such a 'veil of ignorance', people rationally favor social protection, redistributive transfers, progressive taxation as insurance against bad luck. But this argument has recently been challenged with the asssumption that individuals know more and more about their future even at the start of their lives. Based on the social, economic and medical status of one's parents, a large part of future uncertainty can be controlled. As a consequence, this 'behind the

veil' argument is no longer viewed as a good foundation for the welfare state. Or, to put it differently, it explains why the welfare state could eventually shrink and become less and less redistributive.[4]

3. Ethical norm. According to Kant and other philosophers, self-interested individuals could follow a number of ethical norms that are contrary to, or independent of, their immediate interests, and which constrain them in their daily lives. Accordingly, people have two distinct personalities, their self-interested selves being essentially out of joint with their ethical selves. Self-interested preferences guide their day-to-day participation in the market economy, while ethical ones apply to their participation in collective decision-making, including support to the welfare state.[5]

4. Class interest. This is the Marxist view, according to which the welfare state serves the interest of the capitalist class in two ways: by increasing the quantity and quality of the labor force (the reproduction of labor power) and by maintaining social harmony (the reproduction of the relations of production). For example, public health can improve the productivity of the labor force as well as defuse a potential source of tensions.

5. Altruism. Altruism is a hypothesis used by economists to explain why taxpayers are prepared to vote and to pay for some kind of redistribution to the poor. It is better to talk of paternalistic altruism, as it often takes the form of providing the less well-off with specific services or aid, such as health care or food stamps. Implicit to this view is the idea that the tax payers do not trust the poor to spend any transfer in cash wisely.

6. Political economy. Most of the above hypotheses are of a normative nature. They don't really explain why the welfare state is what it is, and whether or not its size and structure are appropriate. To do so, we have to focus on the setting within which political decisions are made. One development within this framework has been the constitutional approach. Accordingly, the desired type of social protection is chosen at a constitutional stage of choice. At this point people are to a considerable extent uncertain about their own position and about the implications of different types of social protection for their own interests. Therefore they may be guided by the kind of consideration that underlines the ethical view just considered, and adopt a criterion of social welfare such as the Rawlsian maximin (maximizing the utility of the worst-off individuals) or the utilitarian sum of individuals' utilities. In the second stage of choice, actual tax rates and benefit levels are governed by the political process, direct or representative democracy, with possible bureaucratic pitfalls.

---

[4] This is at the heart of the 'new social question', developed by Rosenvallon (1995).
[5] This leads to the so-called merit goods.

2 Poverty and inequality

KEY CONCEPTS

Equivalence scale

Gini coefficient

Lorenz curve

poverty gap

poverty line

poverty rate

regression

2.1 Introduction

The failure of the market system to satisfactorily achieve the objectives that our society has set itself is at the heart of the welfare state. This failure is of two types: the 'traditional' market failure that comes from the inability to produce an efficient allocation of resources, and the rather 'normal'[1] failure to provide an equitable outcome. To measure the performance of the market and of the welfare state in terms of equity, we focus on two standard concepts: poverty and inequality.

Poverty and inequality are indeed two ways of characterizing the equity of income distribution. But a number of economists do not want to consider distributional issues at all. According to them any ideas about the right income distribution are value judgments, and there is no scientific way to resolve differences in matters of ethics. The problem with this view is that decision-makers care about the distributional implications of policy. Yet if economists ignore distribution, policymakers may end up paying no attention at all to efficiency, focusing only on distributional issues.

In this chapter we approach the issue of income distribution from the view-point of poverty and inequality. Then we look at the effect of social protection on each one.

2.2 Comparing poverty

In measuring poverty and income inequality, we will focus on the household as the reference unit, and on disposable income as the source of well-being for

---

[1] Normal as long as altruism is assumed away.

the household. To standardize the disposable income of heterogenous households we use an equivalence scale. This is a rather arbitrary choice and it can have implications. The scale recommended by the OECD is used most often in the figures presented here. It assigns a weight of 1.0 to the first adult in a household, 0.7 to each additional adult, and 0.5 to each child. (The equivalent (or standardized) income of a household is obtained by dividing its disposable income by the equivalence scale value, e.g. 2.7 for a couple with two children.)

Income distribution can be considered in terms of its dispersion. Thus one looks at the entire distribution of income. Alternatively, it can be studied by focusing on the bottom of the distribution, that is by the extent of poverty. To measure the level of poverty one traditionally computes the number of households below the 'poverty line', a fixed level of real income considered enough to provide a minimally adequate standard of living. Not surprisingly, there is no agreement on how to determine what is adequate. The poverty lines can be based on basic needs (the cost of minimum food requirements) or on some percentage of mean or median income. The latter approach is based on the idea that poverty is a situation of relative deprivation, and that the poverty line should, therefore, be linked to some indicator of the standard of living in society. We will use this approach which is objective, financial and relative. It is particularly fit for international comparisons. Unless mentioned otherwise, our poverty line will be 50 per cent of median income. In contemplating policies that might alleviate poverty it is sometimes helpful to know just how far below the poverty line the poverty population lies. The 'poverty gap' measures how much income should have to be transferred to the poverty population in order to lift every household up to the poverty line.

Table 2.1 shows the proportion of people below the poverty line (50% of median income) in 15 European countries. In the period 1994–2000, poverty rates range from 3.8 in Denmark to 14.6 in Portugal. One can distinguish countries with relatively low rates (below 7%): Denmark, Finland, Netherlands and Sweden, and those with high rates (above 11%): Ireland, Italy, Spain, Greece and Portugal. This can be contrasted with a rate of 17.2 per cent in the US.

If one were to look in more detail, one would observe the types of individuals who are particularly subject to poverty: young households and female-headed households in which no husband is present. Low educational level and persistent unemployment are also factors of poverty. The size of the family, particularly when no economies of scale are accounted for, also leads to poverty. This pattern of poverty according to household types applies to most European countries. As we see below, the observed poverty levels result from two main sources: the market outcome and the presence and effectiveness of social protection.

Admittedly our approach to poverty is a bit simple. It can only be explained by our concern for international comparisons. Clearly, sociologists tend to

Table 2.1. Income, poverty and inequality in the EU15, 1994–2000

Country	Year	GDP per head (1995 dollars and prices)	Poverty rate (%)	Gini coefficient (%)	Social spending (% of GDP)
Austria	1999	25087	9.3	26.6	26.1
Belgium	1995	21633	7.8	25.0	28.1
Denmark	1994	21975	3.8	26.3	33.1
Finland	2000	23662	6.4	24.7	24.5
France	1994	20461	7.5	28.8	29.3
Germany	2001	23497	10.0	26.4	27.4
Greece	1994	12750	13.9	33.6	21.2
Ireland	2000	27087	15.4	32.3	13.6
Italy	2000	22651	12.9	33.3	24.1
Luxembourg	2000	42310	–	26.0	20.0
Netherlands	2000	25246	6.0	24.8	21.8
Portugal	2000	15592	13.7	–	20.5
Spain	1995	18686	11.5	30.3	21.4
Sweden	2000	24849	5.3	25.2	28.6
United Kingdom	2000	22941	11.4	34.5	21.7
United States	2000	31741	17.2	36.8	14.2

Sources: OECD (2004a, 2004b), LIS (2000), Förster (2003)

go deeper and look for causes. For example, one might wonder what do the long-term unemployed, young people looking for work and on training schemes, single mothers, young couples crippled by the impossibility of paying bills and rent, all have in common? In a recent paper, Castel (2003) puts forward the hypothesis that they express a particular mode of dissociation from the social bond: a disaffiliation. This is a condition of misery different from that of poverty in the strict sense. The latter can perhaps be read as a state, whose forms can be listed in terms of lack (lack of earnings, of housing, of medical care, of education, lack of power or of respect). By contrast, situations of destitution constitute an effect at the place where two vectors meet: one, the axis of integration/non-integration through work; the other, an axis of integration/non-integration into a social and family network. Present-day insecurity largely results from the growing fragility of protective regulations which were implemented from the nineteenth century onwards in order to create a stable situation for workers: the right to work, extended social protection, coverage of social risks set up by the welfare state. Castel describes the specific nature of present-day insecurity as relating to the structure of wage society, its crisis or its disintegration since the mid-1970s. This analysis although very relevant cannot lend itself to straightforward comparisons.

Table 2.2 presents poverty and inequality indices for the mid-nineties and 2000 coming from the three available sources: OECD, Eurostat and the Luxembourg Income Study (LIS). Note that for the poverty rate, the poverty level is 60 per cent of the median income, which explains why the figures are

Table 2.2. Comparison of inequality and poverty indices with three sources, OECD, Eurostat and LIS

		Reference years			Poverty rates 60% median			Ginis		
		OECD	Euro stat	LIS	OECD	Euro stat	LIS	OECD	Euro stat	LIS
Austria	mid-90s	1993	1994	1994	14	13	15	24	27	28
	ca 2000	1999	1999	1997	16	12	14	25	24	27
Belgium	mid-90s	1995	1995	1997	13	15	14	27	28	25
	ca 2000	–	2000	–	–	13	–	–	28	–
Denmark	mid-90s	1994	1994	1995	10	10	17	21	20	26
	ca 2000	2000	2000	–	12	11	–	23	22	–
Finland	mid-90s	1995	1995	1995	11	8	9	23	22	22
	ca 2000	2000	2000	2000	14	11	12	26	24	25
France	mid-90s	1994	1994	1994	14	15	14	28	29	29
	ca 2000	2000	2000	–	13	15	–	27	27	–
Germany	mid-90s	1994	1994	1994	–	15	13	28	27	26
	ca 2000	2001	2001	2000	15	11	13	28	25	25
Greece	mid-90s	1994	1994	–	22	22	–	34	35	–
	ca 2000	1999	1999	–	21	20	–	35	33	–
Ireland	mid-90s	1994	1994	1995	21	19	21	32	33	34
	ca 2000	2000	2000	–	23	21	–	30	29	–
Italy	mid-90s	1995	1995	1995	22	20	21	35	32	34
	ca 2000	2000	2000	2000	20	19	20	35	29	33
Netherlands	mid-90s	1995	1995	1994	14	12	13	26	29	25
	ca 2000	2000	2000	1999	12	11	13	25	26	25
Portugal	mid-90s	1995	1995	–	22	21	–	36	36	–
	ca 2000	2000	2000	–	21	20	–	36	37	–
Spain	mid-90s	1995	1995	–	19	18	–	30	34	–
	ca 2000	–	2000	–	–	19	–	–	33	–
Sweden	mid-90s	1995	1996	1995	8	9	10	21	21	22
	ca 2000	2000	2000	2000	11	10	12	24	24	25
UK	mid-90s	1995	1995	1995	19	18	22	21	32	34
	ca 2000	2000	2000	1999	19	17	21	33	31	35
United States	mid-90s	1995	–	1994	24	–	24	34	–	36
	ca 2000	2000	–	2000	24	–	24	34	–	37

Source: OECD (2005)

higher than those presented in Table 2.1, that are based on a poverty line equal to 50 per cent of the median income. Another noteworthy aspect of Table 2.2 is that it gives an idea of changes in headcount measure of poverty. The (OECD) poverty rate shows an increase over the second half of the 1990s in Austria, Denmark, Finland, Ireland and Sweden while it shows a decline in Italy, France, Greece, the Netherlands, Portugal. There is no change anywhere else, including the US.

Observe that, hopefully, there are no big differences among the three statistical sources. In general we use the OECD sources which are the most complete and include the US for the sake of comparison. Comparing poverty rates for different poverty lines (here 50 and 60% of median income) is quite interesting. A significant share of the population (about 8%) is clustered between the 50 per cent and 60 per cent thresholds. In this book, we focus on one dimension of poverty, the so-called headcount ratio. Another dimension is the income levels of individuals falling below the poverty line. This leads to the so-called poverty gap, which basically indicates the share of aggregate income one would need to get everyone out of poverty. For 2000, this gap ranges from 22 per cent in Finland to 36 per cent in Italy. Over the second half of the 1990s, it declined by more than 5 percentage points in Portugal while increasing considerably in Germany and Ireland (OECD 2005).

2.3 Comparing inequality

The poverty rate as well as alternative measures of poverty focus on a particular population. It is often argued that poverty alleviation is not the sole redistributive objective of social policy, and that insuring that income is more equitably distributed is just as important. There exist a number of summary statistics aimed at compressing a vast amount of information concerning differences in income distributions. These statistics that measure in particular the degree of dispersion or of inequality of peoples' incomes quite often convey value judgements. For example, under some assumptions, and keeping aggregate income constant, more inequality is shown to imply less social welfare.

In this chapter we will use the Gini coefficient as a measure of inequality. To obtain this coefficient, one first compares the cumulative distribution of income to the cumulated distribution of households in the population concerned. This is the Lorenz curve, which plots the percentage of income received by the bottom 20, 30, etc. per cent of the population. If there were full equality, x per cent of the population would receive x per cent of the aggregate income, and then the Lorenz curve would lie along the diagonal of

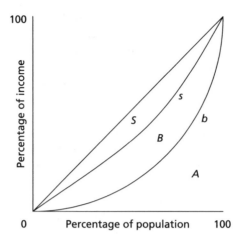

Figure 2.1. Lorenz curves

the diagram in Figure 2.1. The further the curve is away from the diagonal, the further the distribution from full inequality, and therefore the greater the inequality.

The Gini coefficient is calculated by dividing the area between the Lorenz curve and the diagonal, by the area of the triangle formed by the diagonal and the axes. In Figure 2.1, there are two hypothetical Lorenz curves corresponding to two countries: b, for Borduria and s, for Syldavia. The Gini coefficient of Syldavia is equal to the area S divided by the area $S + B + A$ and that of Borduria is equal to $S + B$ divided by $S + B + A$. Clearly, income is more unequally distributed in Borduria than in Syldavia.

Table 2.1 presents the Gini coefficient of EU15 countries plus the United States. As in the case of poverty, one can distinguish two groups of European countries. The Nordic countries, Belgium, Germany, Luxembourg and the Netherlands have the lowest coefficients. By contrast the Anglo-Saxon as well as the Southern countries have the highest coefficients, closer to those of the USA. This clustering is quite similar to that obtained in other studies. As we show in the next section, the ranking of countries by either the Gini coefficient or the head count poverty rate can be explained in part by the differing form and extent of social protection, as well as by the role of redistributive income taxation.

The OECD (OECD 2005, Förster 2003, Burniaux *et al.* 1998, Atkinson 2002, Förster and Pearson 2002) has extensively studied the evolution in income inequality in the last decades. Table 2.2 gives the changes from mid 1990s to 2000. It appears that during that time the Gini coefficient declined in France, Netherlands and Ireland. It remained broadly stable in Germany, Italy and

Portugal. It increased in Austria, Denmark, Greece, the UK, and more significantly in Sweden and Finland. Before 1995 the OECD (2005) distinguishes two periods. From 1975 to 1985 there is little comparable evidence, and for the countries for which it exists no common trend is observed. There is decline in Greece, Finland and Sweden, and increase in the Netherlands and the UK. From 1985 to 1995 there is a clear trend of increased inequality in Austria, Denmark, Greece, UK, Finland and Sweden. Only France and Ireland experienced a slight decrease in inequality.

In spite of these contrasting trends, the overall pattern has not changed much: low inequality in the Nordic countries and the Netherlands and higher inequality in the Anglo-Saxon and the Southern European countries.

2.4 **Redistributive effect of social protection**

The extent of poverty and inequality studied thus far concerns incomes that are net of direct taxes and which include social protection transfers. We now want to look at the impact of such transfers on poverty and inequality. To do so we proceed in two stages, at the aggregate level and at the level of households.

2.4.1 EFFECT ON THE POVERTY OF HOUSEHOLDS

To measure the impact of social protection, we simply compare poverty rates before and after transfers. The practical advantage of this method is that it does not require data on gross income, just on disposable income and on transfers. This is necessary for a number of countries. One major disadvantage of this method is that it overestimates the impact of transfers on poverty. The extent of the bias depends on the level of taxation that low income households pay. Another pitfall of this approach is that it assumes a constant behavior. Indeed it is clear that without some social benefits individuals would change their behavior regarding retirement, work, health treatment, and so on.

The results presented in Table 2.3 and which come from the OECD (see e.g. Förster (2003)) are quite striking. For the most recent period poverty alleviation defined as the difference between poverty before and after transfers ranges from 0.29 in Sweden (1995) to 0.10 in the UK (1995) and in Portugal (2000). What is interesting is the change in poverty alleviation over the two subperiods (1985–95 and 1995–2000). In the chapter on globalization, we will try to relate these changes in poverty alleviation (DAP) to economic integration and factor mobility. For the period 1985–1995 poverty alleviation has increased almost everywhere. For the most recent period 1995–2000, the outcome is mixed. In fact, poverty alleviation decreased in 6 out of 10 countries.

Table 2.3. Poverty alleviation (1985–2000)

	POV	APO	DAP	POV	APO	DAP
Belgium	7.5	26.5	–	–	–	–
Denmark	3.8	21.3	6.5	4.3	18.6	−2.7
Finland	4.9	15.8	6.8	6.4	11.6	−4.2
France	7.5	28.4	4.6	7.0	28.5	0.1
Germany	9.4	16.8	−0.4	10.0	19.3	2.5
Ireland	11.0	23.0	3.3	15.4	15.3	−7.7
Italy	14.2	16.7	6.9	12.9	17.3	0.6
Netherlands	6.3	19.2	−1.5	6.0	16.1	−3.1
Portugal	14.6	11.6	1.9	13.7	10.4	−1.2
Sweden	3.7	29.0	1.7	5.3	21.7	−7.3
United Kingdom	10.9	10.0	−0.3	11.4	17.4	7.4
Period	1995	1995	1985–95	2000	2000	1995–2000

Notes: POV: Poverty rate (50% median income), APO: Poverty alleviation: poverty before minus poverty after transfers, DAP: Increase in poverty alleviation

Source: Förster (2003)

2.4.2 AGGREGATE EFFECT ON POVERTY AND INEQUALITY

Another approach to the same issue is to consider the aggregate relationship between social spending, and either the poverty rate or the inequality measure. To do that we use the data of Table 2.1. Figure 2.2 provides a relationship between poverty rate and social spending. We see clearly that social transfers exert a clear-cut effect on poverty and that there is a strong negative correlation between the two variables.

The results presented in Table 2.4 confirm that larger social expenditure correspond to lower poverty levels. Tests on the time stability of the estimated coefficients suggest that the impact of social transfers on poverty rates has not changed over time.

We should, however, be cautious in interpreting these relations. Indeed they can indicate that social protection 'works.' Yet at the same time, this can simply mean that countries with low poverty rates have a strong preference for social protection. Furthermore, part of the redistribution can be prior to social protection spending. For example, it has been shown that the distribution of wages tends to be more equal in countries with a corporatist setting than in countries where wage is exclusively set by the market. Moreover, we know that corporatist countries tend to have rather generous welfare states. This points to something to which we will return in Chapter 5. Even though this book focuses on the spending side of the welfare state, one should remember that social protection can influence resource allocation and income distribution by other means such as social legislation.

Table 2.4. Impact of social spending on poverty and income inequality (2000)

Dependent variable	Constant	Social spending	R^2
Poverty rate	24.74	−0.616	0.698
	(9.07)	(−5.48)	
Gini coefficient	40.19	−0.474	0.385
	(9.97)	(−2.85)	

Note: *t*-value between brackets

Source: Table 2.1

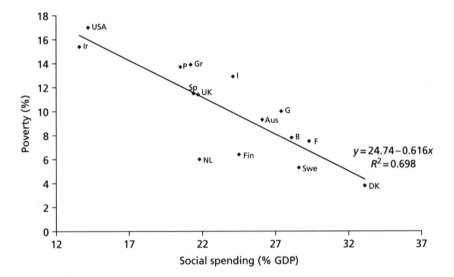

Figure 2.2. Social expenditure and poverty, 1994–2000

Source: Table 2.1

The relation between social protection and an inequality indicator such as the Gini coefficient is not so clear. But it is clearly negative, as shown by Figure 2.3, and the correlation coefficient is equal to about 40 per cent. Table 2.4 gives the regression of the Gini coefficient against social spending. The estimators are quite significant. However, the same reservation made for the poverty rate holds for the indicator of inequality. A society with incomes that are more or less equal can have a strong preference for social protection. Thus the causality link would be reversed. The truth is very likely to be somewhere in between.

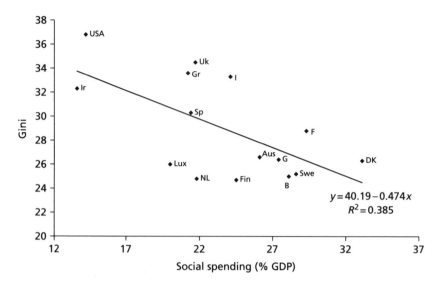

Figure 2.3. Social expenditure and income inequality 1994–2000

Source: Table 2.1

2.4.3 PERMANENT INEQUALITY AND POVERTY ACROSS EUROPEAN COUNTRIES

The comparison presented so far can be criticized because it relies on single-year incomes or earnings. It has long been recognized that there could be high annual income inequality even if the inequality of lifetime (also called permanent) income is very low. The more households move up and down the income ladder throughout their life-cycle, the more single-year inequality will deviate from the inequality of income measured over a longer period of time. As a consequence, if there are differences in income mobility across countries, single-year inequality ranking may yield a misleading picture. Naturally, the same remark applies to poverty measure. In comparison of poverty over time or across countries, instantaneous poverty does not necessarily evolve as persistent poverty.

To illustrate this point, consider two countries in which individuals live for three periods of equal length. Population is constant. In country *A*, each individual earns very little in the first period, but makes up for it in the two following periods. A cross-sectional view of country *A* gives a poverty rate of 33 per cent; in life-cycle terms, everyone is alike and there is no poverty. In country *B*, 20 per cent of the population is persistently poor through the three periods. The others have a constant income. Cross-sectional poverty is thus 20 per cent. This rate is also the rate of persistent poverty.

Table 2.5. Life-cycle income

Periods	Society A			Society B (20%/80%)		
	Generations			Generations		
	t	$t+1$	$t+2$	t	$t+1$	$t+2$
1	10	10	10	10/35	10/35	10/35
2	40	40	40	10/35	10/35	10/35
3	40	40	40	10/35	10/35	10/35
Average cross-sectorial income	30			30		
Average life-time income	30			30		
Cross-sectional poverty	1/3			1/5		
Persistent poverty	0			1/5		
Cross-sectional inequality	2/9			1/9		
Persistent inequality	0			1/9		

This example is presented in Table 2.5. One can easily check that the same conclusion applies for inequality measures. Here we use the coefficient of variation.

It is thus widely agreed that lifetime income, if available, should be used to assess inequality and poverty measures. It could bring a different view supplementing that obtained with income obtained in a given period. Unfortunately, to compare income inequality and poverty across countries on longer time periods than one year requires data that are hardly available. We now examine the existing scanty evidence.

Using longitudinal data sets from four countries, Denmark, Norway, Sweden and the United States, Aaberge *et al.* (2002) look at how the ordering of these countries with respect to income inequality changes when the accounting period is extended from one to several years. They show that the ordering by and large remains unchanged when the period is extended up to 11 years (1980–90). The United States is consistently the most unequal country in spite of a rather high income mobility. They conclude that extending the accounting period and taking account of income mobility have only minor effects on intercountry differences in income inequality.[2] This conclusion is similar to that obtained by Burkhauser and Poupore (1997), Burkhauser *et al.* (1997) in their comparison of Germany and the United States. It is also the same as that of OECD (1996a) that looks at a larger set of countries.

With respect to poverty measurement, research has increasingly focused on persistent income poverty. Using the first three waves of the European Community household panel, Whelan *et al.* (2003) compare for 1995 cross-sectional income poverty at 60 per cent of median income with persistent poverty at 70 per cent of median income. The first ranges from 10.7 per cent in the Netherlands to 21.7 per cent in Portugal and the second from 6.3 per cent

---

[2] See also Bjrklund *et al.* (2002).

in Denmark to 19 per cent in Portugal. Here again the rank correlation between these two indicators is high. Breen and Moisis (2003) use the first four waves of the European Panel. A comparison between poverty rate in wave 4 and the percentage of households being poor in the four waves shows again a rather high correlation. Their main conclusion is that mobility in poverty is highly overestimated if measurement error is ignored.

To conclude, there is no doubt that looking at lifetime income inequality and persistent poverty is important; it brings an alternative viewpoint to the issue of inequality and exclusion. To date, mainly for statistical reasons, there are few studies comparing lifetime income inequality and lifetime income poverty in the European Union countries. Moreover, the existing studies show that the ranking based on yearly income is not much different from that based on lifetime income.

2.5 **Conclusion**

We can now wrap up this chapter on inequality and poverty in the EU, and restate our main findings. First, there are important differences in poverty rates and Gini coefficients across European countries. At the one extreme, there are the Benelux and Nordic countries with little poverty and small inequalities. At the other extreme, there is a mixed group consisting of Southern and of Anglo-Saxon countries. Secondly, part of these differences is attributable to differences in social spending. Thirdly, changes in poverty and inequality over time, have been rather small. Keeping in mind that the most recent figures available are several years old, there are a number of reliable signals pointing to an increase in the near future of poverty and inequality. The main factors leading to this conjecture are unfavorable social and demographic trends, as well as increasingly restrictive public finance.

3 Social spending

KEY CONCEPTS

Entitlement principle   entitlement programs

3.1 Introduction

There is a great diversity among welfare states in the EU. As different systems have developed within the national context mostly after 1945, it is difficult to generalize about a 'European model' of the welfare state. This diversity—which is at the heart of this book—is reflected in the scale of expenditures for social protection systems, the division of expenditures among programs, the structure and design of benefits, the organization and the sources of financing. This chapter deals with the first two points. We first look at the level and structure of expenditures for the last year for which data is available. Then, we turn to the evolution of social expenditure over time. The financing issue is dealt with in Chapter 4. We discuss the issue of comparison of social expenditures across countries and consider the problem of entitlement that explains why dismantling programs that have lost their relevancy is so difficult.

3.2 Level and profile

The level of expenditure on welfare states in Europe for year 2001 varies between 29.2 per cent of GDP in Denmark and 13.8 per cent in Ireland, as shown in Table 3.1. This lower bound is hardly below the 14.8 per cent in the US. The figures for Sweden, France and Denmark are quite above this average. By contrast, expenditures in Ireland, the Netherlands, Luxembourg, Spain, Portugal and the UK are below this average. It is tempting to check whether there is a relation between social protection and GDP per head. For decades there was a tendency for the richer countries to have the largest welfare states. Lately, this relation has disappeared, as Figures 3.1(a) and (b) show.

Countries with more or less the same GDP show a wide range of behavior. This new pattern is good news. When there was a clear relation between

Table 3.1. Total expenditure for social protection as a percentage of GDP, 1980, 1990 and 2001

Country	1980	1990	2001
Austria	22.5	24.1	26.0
Belgium	24.1	26.9	27.2
Denmark	29.1	29.3	29.2
Finland	18.5	24.8	24.8
France	21.1	26.6	28.5
Germany	23.0	22.8	27.4
Greece	11.5	20.9	24.3
Ireland	17.0	18.6	13.8
Italy	18.4	23.3	24.4
Luxembourg	23.5	21.9	20.8
Netherlands	26.9	27.6	21.8
Portugal	10.9	13.9	21.1
Spain	15.9	19.5	19.6
Sweden	28.8	30.8	28.9
United Kingdom	17.9	19.5	21.8
EU15	20.6	23.4	24.0
United States	13.3	13.4	14.8

Source: OECD (2004a)

social spending and GDP, one was facing a 'chicken or egg' causality problem. At the same time one could argue that higher spending leads to higher national income, and conversely that successful countries with high income per head can afford generous social protection. We shall come back to this question, as it has some bearing on the alleged depressive effect of social protection on economic performance. At this point we will simply note that today there is no such relation between social protection and GDP. When there was one, one could have hypothesized that the industrialization of the economy and the ensuing social changes led to both higher levels of income and to the need for more social protection. Industrialization made life uncertain; at the same time, it forced out traditional insurance mechanisms such as the family at large.

The breakdown of total social expenditures into individual programs reveals interesting similarities and specificities, as presented in Table 3.2.

Pension benefits account for the largest share of social expenditures in welfare states, this level being particularly high in Italy and Greece, and particularly low in Ireland. The second largest component is health care: above 40 per cent in Ireland, Luxembourg, the Netherlands, Sweden, the UK and Portugal, and equal or below 30 per cent in Greece and Austria. Together social security and health care account for over 75 per cent of social spending in most European countries, the only exception being Finland and Denmark.

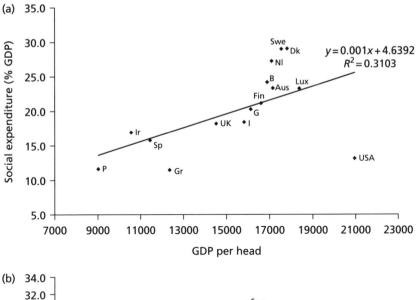

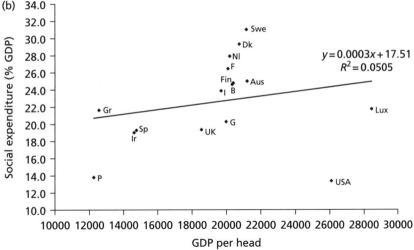

Figure 3.1. Social spending and GDP per head, (a) 1980, (b) 1990

Sources: Table 3.1 and OECD (2004b)

For the other functions, there is a large diversity that can be explained by social policy objectives. Unemployment benefits reach 15.3 per cent in Denmark, but are negligible in Greece, the UK, Italy and Luxembourg. Maternity and housing benefits represent more than 15 per cent of social spending in Denmark, Ireland and the UK; they are very small in Portugal, Spain and Italy.

Table 3.2. Social protection benefits by function, 2003

Country	Health	Old age	Family/housing	Labour market	Others	Total
Austria	30.0	51.6	11.6	4.9	1.9	100
Belgium	35.6	41.5	8.5	12.9	1.5	100
Denmark	37.4	28.5	15.2	15.3	3.6	100
Finland	36.9	35.8	13.4	11.8	2.1	100
France	32.8	42.7	12.9	10.2	1.4	100
Germany	37.7	44.1	7.7	8.6	1.9	100
Greece	28.9	55.7	10.6	2.3	2.5	100
Ireland	45.8	25.2	15.4	10.2	3.5	100
Italy	34.5	56.8	4.1	4.4	0.1	100
Luxembourg	40.0	38.8	17.1	3.1	1.0	100
Netherlands	44.9	32.4	6.9	12.9	2.9	100
Portugal	41.8	44.4	5.5	7.1	1.2	100
Spain	39.4	45.3	3.5	11.0	0.8	100
Sweden	43.6	34.0	12.3	8.0	2.2	100
United Kingdom	39.5	39.9	16.9	2.9	0.9	100
United States	49.7	41.4	2.6	3.1	3.2	100

Source: OECD (2004a)

3.3 **Evolution**

A number of articles and books recently published talk of the dismantlement (Pierson (1997)),[1] the rolling back (Atkinson (2000)) of the welfare state. In this section, we try to determine to what extent this scenario has been borne out over the last decades.

Real social expenditures increase in all countries. But this upward movement proves to be far from homogenous across time and countries. In any case, the most relevant comparison must concern social spending in percentage of GDP, sometimes labelled 'social burden' for short.

Globally the social burden goes up in all countries over the period 1980–1998, except in Ireland, Luxembourg and the Netherlands. But time trends are not linear. In broad outline, after a stagnation from 1985 to 1989, average social burden increases from 1989 to 1993 and declines slightly afterwards. From 1980 to 1998, as shown by Table 3.1, it increases from 21 per cent to 24.1 per cent in EU15. This might be compared with the US, where it increases from 13.1 to 14.6.

---

[1] Pierson (2001) is one of the political scientists in favor of the so-called 'new politics' of the welfare states. His view focuses on two factors limiting the decline of welfare states: the popularity of the welfare state and the existence of formal and informal institutional veto forces. As a consequence, he finds evidence supporting the effects of little partisan politics. In contrast, there is another school of thought adopting the 'amended' power resources approach for which partisan politics plays a decisive role in the decline of modern welfare states. Korpi and Palma (2003) adopt this view in their analysis of the British case.

Beyond a number of national differences, it is nevertheless possible to statistically identify three rather homogeneous subgroups[2] in EU15. Homogeneity is measured in terms of level of and change in social burden.

- High spending countries (Belgium, Denmark, Finland, France, Germany, the Netherlands and Sweden) display both the largest social spending rates and per capita incomes of the Union, with the smallest changes in those two indicators.

- Medium spending countries (Germany, Ireland, Italy, Luxembourg and the United Kingdom) with their economic and social characteristics, levels and changes, lie halfway between those of the other two subgroups.

- Low spending countries (Greece, Portugal and Spain) remaining 'laggards' in terms of social protection and economic development, while experiencing the highest growth rates in both variables (particularly Greece and Portugal). This is illustrated in Figure 3.2 with the thick line representing the EU15 average evolution.

What have been the implications of those contrasted evolutions for existing international differences? The usual statistics and econometric tests show that they have markedly declined over time (see Table 3.3). On the one hand, the 25 per cent increase in the minimum to maximum ratio (from 37% to 47%) indicates that the gap between extreme social expenditure rates has fallen somewhat since 1985. It reached a peak in 1996. On the other hand, there has been a certain reduction in the overall range of the EU social burden, as denoted by the fall in the coefficient of variation (from 21 to 18).

This reduction in dispersion results mainly from the fact that less generous social systems (Greece, Portugal, Spain and Italy) in the early eighties experienced globally higher growth rates than more thriving systems (Northern states). The existence of such a converging scheme is widely supported by the strong negative correlation between the initial social burden and the subsequent growth rate as well as by the regression presented in Table 3.3. As one observes, the convergence is sharper in EU15 than in the whole set of OECD countries.

To sum up, social burdens in the Union have been following a converging and globally increasing path since 1980, with some stagnation since 1993. In the chapters devoted to specific social spending, we shall see whether these evolutions can be explained by an increase in risk related to that particular spending. For example, one would expect the evolution in unemployment benefits to be linked to the rate of unemployment, and the evolution in social security spending to the increase in the dependency ratio. Figure 3.3 indicates that all functions except unemployment insurance have increased quite smoothly.

---

[2] The F-test indicates that subgroup mean values are significantly different from each other for each year and for the entire period.

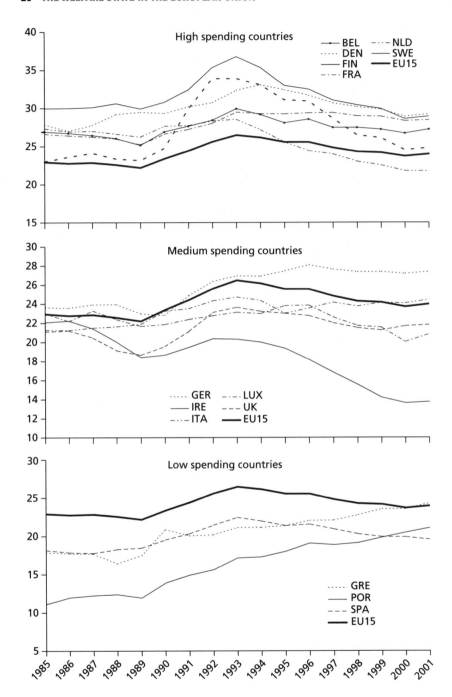

Figure 3.2. Social spending as a share of GDP, 1980–2001

Source: OECD (2004a)

Table 3.3. Convergence of social spending (1985–2001)

Year	Min/Max ratio	Coefficient of variation
1985	37.12	20.81
1986	39.93	20.70
1987	40.64	20.87
1988	40.47	22.33
1989	39.95	22.24
1990	45.16	19.27
1991	46.02	19.67
1992	44.23	20.91
1993	46.71	20.49
1994	48.94	19.98
1995	54.69	18.20
1996	55.95	17.68
1997	54.18	17.38
1998	51.16	17.65
1999	47.45	18.15
2000	47.16	17.73
2001	47.07	17.65
	Initial social spending and subsequent annual growth rate	
EU15		
Correlation coefficient	−0.70	
Regression		
constant	23.39	(21.38)
slope	−0.12	(−3.14)
OECD		
Correlation coefficient	−0.69	
Regression		
constant	21.23	(19.67)
slope	−0.03	(−4.46)

Note: t-statistics between brackets

3.4 **Problems of comparison**

Throughout this book we use social expenditure data made comparable over time and across countries by both OECD and Eurostat. Yet, this data may fail to reflect the true effort of a country in providing social support during a given year. Account needs to be taken of the effects of tax systems and transfers which, although mandatory, are not paid by government. In other words, ideally, we should use a net rather than a gross concept of social expenditure. To do so, various delicate adjustments to raw data are needed. When correcting for differences in tax and institutional arrangements, it appears that some international disparities are less sharp than they appear at first sight.

Following Adema *et al.* (1996) and Adema (1999, 2001), let us illustrate four examples where adjustments are needed. To do so we consider two fictitious countries: Borduria and Syldavia.

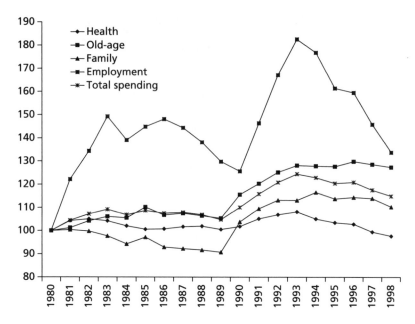

Figure 3.3. Real growth of social spending by functions at the EC level (1980=100)
Source: OECD (2001a)

- Borduria and Syldavia have a sickness benefit program involving con-tributions by employers to a social insurance fund as well as payments from that fund to qualified individuals. Borduria decides to abolish this program and by law to force employers to make payments to qualified individuals. As a consequence, social spending falls in Borduria relatively to Syldavia.
- Borduria and Syldavia don't tax social security benefits. Borduria decides to impose the regular income tax to retirees, but to increase their benefits so as to keep their net income unchanged. Social spending increases in Borduria.
- Borduria's social security system consists of a meager flat benefit, but it gives large tax advantages on contributions to private pensions plan. As a consequence, social security spending is much lower in Borduria than in Syldavia even though the total flow of public money is the same in the two countries.
- Borduria and Syldavia are identical economies in all respect, except that Borduria experiences a great deal of volatility in GDP. As a consequence, social spending is much higher in Borduria in a period of cyclical bust, than in Syldavia, because of a higher demand for unemployment benefits.

Table 3.4 gives some preliminary results of these adjustments for 10 coun-tries. It can be seen that the differences in gross direct social spending are

Table 3.4. Gross to net social spending
as a percentage of GDP, 1997

Country	Gross	Net
Austria	28.5	23.4
Belgium	30.4	26.3
Denmark	35.9	26.7
Finland	33.3	24.8
Germany	29.2	27.2
Ireland	19.6	17.1
Italy	29.4	24.1
Netherlands	27.1	20.3
Sweden	35.7	28.5
United Kingdom	23.8	21.6
United States	15.8	16.4

Source: Adema (2001)

larger than after adjustments in social spending. However, one should note that if two countries provide the same amount of social spending in net terms, this does not mean that the two systems have the same allocative and distributive effects.

3.5 **The entitlement problem**

It is somehow surprising to observe that in almost all EU countries, even the high spenders, social spending as a percentage of GDP is increasing. As we see below, there are a number of factors acting against such an evolution. The main reason for the continuous increase of the social burden is the growth of entitlements.

Entitlements are government programs providing funds to those who qualify, rather than appropriating a fixed amount of money for a program. For example, unemployment compensation is paid to those unemployed individuals who qualify; there is no set budget for the program (although there is an estimate of how much the program will cost). Entitlement spending is sometimes referred to as uncontrollable, because once the program is in effect, the level of expenditures depends upon external conditions. As a matter of routine, recent entitlement expenditures have exceeded estimates in all sectors of social protection, except family allowances. But this has not always been the case. In the beginning of social protection, programs made surpluses that were accumulated in funds.

The fact is that entitlement program spending is really not uncontrollable. At any time public authorities can raise the eligibility requirements for any program, modify it, or cancel it altogether. But in order to do that, they face powerful lobbies. Cutting back entitlement programs when costs can be displaced onto future generations is particularly harsh in terms of political feasibility.

We shall come back to this difficulty that is at the center of the crisis of the welfare state, and specifically of the social security systems.

3.6 **Conclusion**

This chapter has provided an overview of the level, pattern and evolution of social spending in the European Union. Even though one observes some convergence, social spending is increasing in almost all countries. One of the reasons for this is the development of entitlements that make it difficult to dismantle programs that have lost most of their *raison d'être*. Another issue discussed was that of the international comparison of programs that are public in some countries and private, but heavily subsidized, in others.

4 Revenue sources

4.1 Introduction

In this chapter we look at the alternative sources of financing social protection in the European Union. The main source is payroll taxation. Two issues are often raised: that of the regressivity of payroll taxation and that of enlarging a tax base that is increasingly restricted to salaried work.

4.2 Financing the welfare state

There are a number of sources of finance to welfare states in European countries. These include:

- General tax revenue—direct and indirect taxes
- Employer/employee social insurance contributions—either earmarked for individual programs or put in a general fund to finance the social protection system as a whole
- Special taxes—e.g. energy tax or income tax surcharges forming a 'solidarity contribution' towards the finance of social protection systems
- Direct charges and fees for public goods and services
- Tax expenditures—e.g. tax breaks towards private education, health insurance and pension schemes.

Table 4.1 presents the structure and the evolution of social protection financing EU12. Together, employer and employee social insurance contributions form the largest source of finance in European countries. In 2000, employers' and employees' contributions accounted for more than 70 per cent of total receipts of social protection in the majority of countries. Notable exceptions

Table 4.1. Financing of social protection

		Bel	Den	Fra	Ger	Gre	Ire	Ita	Lux	Nld	Por	Spa	UK
Employers' contributions	1980	44.5	10.0	55.5	41.5	57.8	24.6	59.9	35.4	37.1	53.2	63.6	33.4
	1990	43.7	7.2	50.4	42.2	38.1	24.0	52.6	29.8	20.1	41.8	–	27.9
	2000	49.5	9.1	45.9	36.9	38.2	25.0	43.2	24.6	29.1	35.9	39.7	30.2
Employees' contributions	1980	17.8	2.3	24.3	28.0	31.2	11.2	13.9	23.4	31.0	18.7	18.8	14.6
	1990	25.7	4.5	28.3	28.3	20.3	15.0	16.1	22.1	40.3	19.1	–	25.8
	2000	22.8	20.3	20.6	28.2	22.6	15.1	14.9	23.8	38.8	17.6	9.4	21.4
General government contributions	1980	34.0	82.9	17.3	26.9	4.7	63.3	23.8	32.8	20.4	25.4	16.1	43.2
	1990	21.4	81.7	17.6	26.9	32.8	60.0	29.1	40.6	23.9	26.1	–	44.6
	2000	25.3	63.9	30.6	32.5	29.1	58.3	39.8	47.1	14.2	38.7	46.7	47.1
Other	1980	3.8	4.7	2.9	3.6	6.2	1.0	2.4	8.4	11.5	2.7	1.5	8.7
	1990	9.2	6.6	3.6	2.6	8.8	1.0	2.2	7.5	15.7	13.0	–	1.7
	2000	2.5	6.7	2.9	2.4	10.1	1.5	2.1	4.5	17.9	7.8	4.3	1.3

Source: Eurostat (2003), European Social Statistics, Social Protection Expenditures and Receipts, 1991–2000

were Denmark, Ireland, and to a lesser extent the UK and Portugal, where general tax revenue forms a large share of finance. One should note that this prevailing financing structure is at the heart of a social protection program based on the labor market and co-managed by unions and employers. Thus it is not surprising to see Ireland and the UK as outliers in this respect as in many others. It is more surprising to see Denmark, and to a lesser degree Portugal, adopt a different financing structure relative to the other member states.

In the case of social spending, we have spoken of convergence. We can also speak of converging trends in the financing of social protection: increase in the tax-financed component, reduction in employer contributions, particularly for certain categories of workers (young, unskilled). The share of government funds, as opposed to wage related contributions, is increasing regularly in the majority of countries. This trend, known as one of 'fiscalization' is particularly evident in the Southern European countries and Luxembourg. Along the same line, some countries have introduced a new 'solidarity tax' in an attempt to make up deficits in social protection programs. The creation of the CSG (Contribution Sociale Généralisée) in France, and of the Solidarity Payroll Tax in Belgium, is an attempt to widen the tax base upon which social protection schemes are traditionally funded. These new taxes are supposed to reach capital income and replacement income, in particular.

The share of employer contributions has fallen a lot, particularly in countries where that share was important. The pressure for further reduction is mounting. Reforms have focused on selective cuts. Problems of unemployment have prompted reductions in contributions for low-income earners and young workers. These cuts are observed in France, Belgium, Ireland and the UK. Paradoxically, the trend towards fiscalization is sometimes coupled with a trend towards developing actuarial schemes, whereby contributions and benefits are closely linked, as in private insurance. This is particularly true in the area of pensions and health care. We will come back to this evolution towards a two-tier system of social protection: social assistance financed by general revenue and ensuring a flat benefit to all and actuarially fair schemes that are often, but not necessarily, private.

4.3 **Alternative sources**

The various effects of labor-specific employer and employee social insurance contributions are the subject of various debates and of a large number of studies. Labor-specific taxes are often deemed to be regressive and to hurt competitiveness and employment. As a consequence, governments are increasingly searching for alternative sources of finance, notably through the fiscalization of social systems. Their hope is to have a financing structure that is less regressive, that implies fewer disincentives and that rests on a wider base than the current one.

4.3.1 REGRESSIVE TAXATION

From a purely public finance viewpoint, a payroll tax is just a flat tax on labor income. In some countries there are ceilings: that is, earnings levels beyond which the marginal tax rate falls to zero. Compared to a progressive personal income tax, for example, such a payroll tax is less redistributive. Not only is the relative tax burden the same for low and average wage earners, but it may decrease for high wage earners when there is a ceiling. Given that the share of wage earnings that comprises the income of a household decreases as income increases, one sees that payroll taxation is as regressive as consumption taxation.

4.3.2 ADVERSE EFFECT ON COMPETITION

It is also argued that financing social protection from labor-specific taxes has an adverse effect on a nation's competitiveness. Payroll taxes add to a firm's wage costs and costs of production. The higher this burden, the less competitive that firm will be relative to firms from countries with lower tax burdens. This argument is linked to the notions of fiscal competition and social dumping (to which we will come back in Chapter 6) and whereby investment decisions are heavily influenced by the cost of labor input. This argument holds in particular with unskilled, low-wage labor that suffers from competition with countries having lower levels of social protection and lower labor costs. It has led a number of EU countries to introduce payroll tax cuts for unskilled labor.

At this point two remarks are in order. They pertain to the concept of tax shifting and to the benefit side of taxation. In theory, any increase in labor-specific taxes in perfectly competitive labor and product markets would have no impact on unemployment and wage costs. Any attempt by workers to compensate for higher taxes through higher wage demands would push up unemployment levels, driving wages back down again. In the real world, however, product and labor markets are not perfectly competitive. Higher wage demands may be passed on to consumers, wages do not clear automatically; and the final result of the wage-bargaining process depends on the relative strength of the position of employers and employees. Unemployment is not a simple function of wage costs; it has a number of other causes and influences. This is particularly true for unskilled labor, where real wages cannot adjust downwards because of the minimum wage prevailing in a number of countries.

Once again, in theory and in a Robinson Crusoe economy, one would expect that for each Euro of contribution there would be a Euro of benefit, and that such a one-to-one relation would neutralize any adverse effect of social insurance contribution. We will see that for a number of reasons this one-to-one relation does not really hold. But rather in some cases, it turns out to be a one-to-nothing relation.

4.3.3 A SHRINKING TAX BASE

There is another reason why governments have become increasingly concerned over the growing share of tax on labor as a way to finance social protection, and more generally public expenditure. The share of regular, steady salaried labor is declining in a large number of countries, and thus the share of payroll tax base in the GDP is shrinking. As a result, governments are searching for alternative sources of finances. At the risk of being overly simplistic in our view of national accounts, we could say that on the expenditure side there are two main components: consumption, C, and savings, S. On the income side there are: wage earnings, W, other sources of earnings (self-employed, informal work), E, and capital income, K, to which one adds social benefits, B, and substracts direct taxes, T. We write national income, Y, net of tax:

$$Y - T = C + S = W + E + K + B - T$$

As just mentioned, the share of wage earnings in national income (W/Y) is decreasing. At the same time, social protection caters to individuals who have no direct relationship to the regular wage market: non-working spouses, children, informal workers, unemployed, and so on. These individuals benefit from social protection without contributing to it, at least directly or sufficiently.

In a report of the European Commission (EC 1996), one finds that over the last decade labor-specific taxes, that is, social insurance contribution and personal income taxation applied to earnings, have increased as a source of government revenue. The tax burden on other-than-labor factors of production has decreased during the same period. More precisely in the period 1980–93 the European average of the implicit tax rate has increased from 35 per cent to 41 per cent for labor employed, and decreased from 46 per cent to 40 per cent for other factors of production (capital, labor self-employed, energy, national resources), and been stable at around 13 per cent for public and private consumption. One is thus faced with the simple question: why can't we find serious alternative sources of finance to public and social spending?

Let us briefly consider some potential tax bases.

- Consumption taxes.
  These are surely the most serious alternative. By increasing taxes such as VAT, the tax burden falls on consumers rather than on workers and on

producers. People who receive an income from capital are also contributing to tax revenue. The disadvantages are that flat rate consumption taxes are already widely used in the EU, and that they tend to be regressive, slightly more and differently than payroll taxes.

- Taxes on capital.
  Capital income and profits are subject to rather low taxes in the EU. There are two main reasons for this. First, as we shall see, tax competition is particularly strong for this type of tax. The second reason is that taxation of financial capital, as opposed to real estate, can easily be avoided, if not evaded.

- Tax on self-employment.
  The issue of compliance also explains why effective taxation on self-employment, and on informal activities is low.

- Tax on replacement incomes.
  Social protection benefits are less and less tax exempted at least beyond a minimum level. In an ageing society where elderly people benefit from incomes as high as those of other age groups, imposing taxes at least partially is increasingly accepted. This is an indirect way to tax income from occupational pensions, life insurance and other forms of savings.

To sum up, there is not much of an alternative to payroll taxation. The only tax base that seems to resist erosion is either the wage bill or final consumption. Both concern the same people. As a consequence, the alternative seems to be something between a regressive payroll tax and another, but differently, regressive value added tax. It is important to note that the choice of a source of finance has implications, not only in terms of efficiency and equity, but also in terms of organization. Countries which move away from wage related contributions also move away towards a more centralized state-managed organization from a 'corporatist' conception of social protection, that is a set of programs jointly managed by employees and employers.

4.4 Social insurance contributions

In a large number of countries, social insurance contributions have long been considered as distinct from other sources of finance. In the beginning they were sufficient to finance social insurance. Indeed, it was possible to create funds to be used in case of bad times. Social insurance contributions were sometimes, and still are, divided according to function: family allowances, retirement, unemployment to generate distinct funds. Today most funds are depleted and these distinctions are at best formal.

The specificity of social insurance contributions can be explained in two ways. First, social insurance was co-managed by employee unions and employer organizations; together they decide the amount of benefits, contribution rates and investment in funds. Secondly, social contributions were viewed as totally different from taxes. Because they were earmarked and because the amount of contributions paid by a worker determined the amount of his/her benefits, contributions (also called payroll taxes) were considered as quasi-premiums, quasi-prices rather than taxes.

There are few empirical studies that try to assess the perception workers and employers have of these payroll taxes. Conventionally contributions to social insurance are treated as pure taxes, for example, in calculations of the tax wedges by OECD. But this approach ignores any future rights to benefits perceived as such by contributors. In fact, social benefits contain both an actuarial and a redistributive component, the relative importance of which depends on whether the system is more or less contributive.[1] Recently all this has changed, which may be due to the idea that payroll taxes are less and less viewed as premiums even when benefits are related to payments. The share of contributions decreases consistently; (central) governments are taking over the organization and the management of social protection. As a consequence, more and more contributions are viewed as taxes. We will come back to this important issue. Indeed, if payroll contributions are considered to be taxes, that is, if they have the same distortionary effects as any other income tax, even when benefits are totally linked to these contributions, then the case for social insurance weakens.

4.5 Conclusion

Payroll taxation is still today the main source of financing social protection in the European Union. Ireland and Denmark are the only exceptions. In most countries, payroll taxation is an integral part of the social insurance compact which involves unions and management. Payroll taxes are often presented as contributions or premiums paid for an insurance service. However whether it is so perceived by workers is an open question.

---

[1] See 5.2.1 on this point.

5 Types of social protection

Active welfare state
actuarial principle
categorical benefits
decommodification
earnings-related benefits

flat-rate benefits
means-tested benefits
poverty trap
workfare

5.1 Introduction

There does not exist a single model of welfare state in the European Union. Each country has its own model that is the result of its political and social culture and of its economic evolution. There exists a number of taxonomies of welfare states which focus on specific features of their functioning. We focus on a taxonomy based on two characteristics: the generosity and the redistributiveness of programs. The main interest of distinguishing among types of social protection programs is the different implications they have in terms of efficiency, equity and political sustainability.

5.2 Taxonomy of social protection

Most social protection systems include a mixture of transfers that differ by being either in cash or in kind, and by a type of benefit formula. One distinguishes three basic formulas: means-tested benefits, flat-rate benefits, and earnings-related benefits, to which one could add public subsidies for the purchase of private goods or services.

To receive a means-tested benefit, a family has to show that its income—its means—falls below a certain level. Welfare compensations such as the RMI (Revenu Minimum d'Insertion) in France, the Minimex in Belgium or the Supplementary Benefit in the UK are typical means-tested transfers paid to those with low incomes and not working.

There are two non-means-tested formulas, also called categorical. Categorical benefits are paid to all those who fall within a particular category (the

Table 5.1. Taxonomy of social transfers

	Means tested	Categorical	
		Flat benefits (universalistic, Beveridgean)	Earnings-related benefits (social insurance, Bismarkian)
In cash	Welfare compensation	Family allowances	Unemployment compensation
In nature	Food stamps	Health services	–

elderly, families with children, the unemployed, and so on) regardless of their income. The first categorical benefits are those that are uniform, that is, unrelated to past contributions. One also speaks of 'universalistic' programs as providing equal benefits: equal access to health care to all, or child allowances that go to all families with children.

The second type of categorical benefits are the earnings-related benefits. There are indeed a number of programs that pay benefits that depend on past income or contributions. Table 5.1 presents those different types of programs. Even though all European countries employ policies of all types, the mixture can differ dramatically.

To cite one example, the US government spends as much as most European governments on health care. However, there is a large difference in the design of health care policies. In most European countries health care is a universalistic benefit-equal program care for all. By contrast in the US, health care public expenditures are divided into a universalistic program for the elderly (medicare), a means-tested program for the poor (medicaid) and tax subsidies for private health care for the private sector employees.

In 'The Three Worlds of Welfare Capitalism', Esping-Andersen (1990) distinguishes among three different types of welfare state, that he calls *welfare state regimes*, and which correspond to three different mixtures of benefit formula and generosity in spending.[1]

First, there is the 'liberal' welfare state where means-tested assistance predominates. Benefits accrue mainly to a clientele of low-income households. In countries that adopt this welfare state regime, entitlement rules are strict and often associated with stigma, while benefits are typically modest. The archetypal examples of this model are the USA, Canada and Australia. The second welfare state regime clusters nations such as Austria, France,

---

[1] See also Svallfors (1997) who analyses attitudes to redistribution and income differences in eight Western nations and on that basis develops his own taxonomy of welfare states: the social democratic (Sweden/Norway), the conservative (German/Austria), the liberal (US/Canada) and the radical (Australia/New Zealand).

Germany and Italy. They are strongly 'corporatist', above the market forces and attached to class and status. Their welfare states leave little room for private insurance and are hardly redistributive. The third welfare state regime caters to 'social democratic' countries, such as the Scandinavian ones, in which the principle of universalism of social rights prevails. It tends to be rather generous and redistributive, and committed to a heavy social-service burden.

Esping-Andersen (1990) uses the concept of 'de commodification' of social protection, meaning that services are rendered and transfers made as a matter of right, without reliance on the market. Using a number of indicators, he builds a scale of decommodification and rates his sample of welfare states accordingly. Table 5.2 ranks 12 nations according to their decommodification score.[2] This allows him to distinguish among three welfare state regimes: the Anglo-Saxon 'new' nations are all concentrated at the bottom of his index; the Scandinavian countries are at the top; in between, we find the continental European countries some of which, like Belgium and the Netherlands, fall close to the Nordic cluster.

Note that the ranking of countries is likely to vary according to the programs at hand. Furthermore, Esping-Andersen's is not the only type of clustering. Another distinction often made is between Bismarckian and Beveridgean systems (Purton 1996). In the first, contributions through employment generate entitlement to benefits, and benefits are closely linked to occupations and income. The Beveridgean system, on the other hand, ensures that all individuals belonging to some category are entitled to a basic level of income at a flat rate

Table 5.2. The rank role of welfare state. Decommodification scores

Country	Score
United States	13.8
Ireland	23.3
United Kingdom	23.4
Italy	24.1
France	27.5
Germany	27.7
Finland	29.2
Austria	31.1
Belgium	32.4
Netherlands	32.4
Denmark	38.1
Sweden	39.1

Source: Esping-Andersen (1990)

[2] Esping-Andersen in fact ranks 18 countries. Table 5.2 considers only European countries and the United States.

and independent of income. This distinction, widely used, in some circles is a bit surprising. Beveridge had originally argued that everyone should pay the same contribution and receive the same benefit. Bismarck, on the other hand, was in favor of an earnings-related benefit scheme, but without assistance features. There is naturally some overlap between Esping-Andersen's three regimes, and the Beveridge-Bismarck dichotomy. Actually, the rate of decommodification increases with the generosity (size of spending) and the redistributiveness of the system (how Beveridgean it is).

But why are we concerned with such a taxonomy? There are at least three reasons. Depending on the welfare state regime, the implications on income inequality and poverty, on incentives and on political sustainability may vary a lot. Before looking at these three implications, it is important to note that a social protection system can be defined by its degree of redistributiveness and by its generosity. The first one is characterized by the level of flat benefit awarded to everyone, or by the parameters of means-testing. The second one can be proxied by the share of spending to GDP. This distinction is quite important when comparing countries. In the above distinction of welfare state regimes, the 'Nordic' and the 'Anglo-Saxon' regimes are both redistributive, but the former are by far more generous.

5.3 Implications of alternative regimes

5.3.1 REDISTRIBUTION

Consider a given amount of resources. How can it be best allocated if the main purpose is poverty relief? Clearly, a means-tested transfer program prevails over a flat benefit scheme, and surely over an earnings-related benefit scheme. Conversely, a pure earnings-related benefit scheme has no effect on poverty or even on income inequality. One way to assess the effect of alternative systems on poverty is to calculate what has been termed their 'vertical expenditure efficiency', that is, the proportion of the benefits that accrue to households that would have been poor in the absence of benefits.[3]

Paradoxically, it has been observed that a number of means-tested programs have poor vertical efficiency (Beckerman and Clark 1982). This explains why some egalitarian and social protection reformers argue for a 'Back to Beveridge' approach. In other words they favor universalistic rather than means-tested programs. They do so because of two major disadvantages of means-tests: their relative low take-up and their high administrative cost. People eligible for means-tested benefits often do not apply for them partly because of a lack of

---

[3] This is close to the effect of social protection on poverty and inequality studied in Chapter 3.

knowledge, partly because of a reluctance to accept what may be perceived as charity,[4] and partly because of the complex administrative procedures involved. Universalistic benefits often have 100 per cent take up. They also cost less, as they don't imply any control of admissibility, except for the category involved.

5.3.2 INCENTIVES

The three benefits rules: means-tested, flat-rate and earnings-related are also very different with respect to their effects on the incentive to work. All forms of social protection create some disincentive to work. On the revenue side, the payroll tax, or any other tax, implies some allocative distortion. On the benefit side, payments mean that their recipients have to work less hard to obtain a given standard of living. In the terminology of Chapter 7, increased resources (the income effect) discourage work. Means-tested benefits have a built in additional disincentive, for they always involve a reduction in benefit if the individual concerned works harder, and thus raises his or her means of support. The gains from substituting work for leisure are reduced. Put another way, individuals face a marginal tax on their earnings that can go above 100 per cent: for every Euro earned, more than one Euro is taken away in benefits (welfare payment, housing subsidy, school lunch, etc.). This situation is often termed 'poverty trap', that is to say, a situation where there is no net financial gain by working. This may explain part of the current unemployment in the EU and has led to corrective measures in the spirit of the EITC (Earned Income Tax Credit) in the United States, namely an employment subsidy.

Note, however, that some categorical benefits are also subject to the same disincentive effects as means-tested benefits. When the category is somewhat manipulable, there can be an incentive to belong to it in order to get benefits. Disability and unemployment are typical of such categories. In the Netherlands where disability compensations were relatively high and disability tests rather loose, the percentage of disabled workers just before retirement exceeded an astonishing 1/2 for several years.

Conversely, earnings related benefits are expected to bring less disincentive effects than universalistic benefits. The reason is simple. Assume a payroll tax of rate τ and an earnings related scheme that gives back k percent of earnings ($k < \tau$) to the individual concerned. If this individual really understands the relation between contributions and benefits, his or her effective tax rate will drop to $\tau - k$, instead of τ that would be the tax rate of a universalistic program with the same generosity. On the other hand, the higher k, the lower the program redistributiveness. We thus come back to the equity–efficiency quandary.

---

[4] One speaks of stigmatization.

In a Bismarckian system, even a partial one, the relevant question is whether or not contributors perceive that what they pay will be returned to them at least in part. As yet there has been little work on this. Recently, Disney (2004) has tried to split between the Beveridgean (tax) and the Bismarckian (premium) component in social security benefits across a range of OECD countries and time periods. He has found that the Beveridgean component has an adverse effect on the activity of women, but not of men.[5] In the French tradition, the concept of solidarity is widely used to characterize a welfare state of the Bismarckian type. One of the alleged properties of a solidarity welfare state is that it provides a lot of insurance and little redistribution, but in a way that is widely accepted by everyone; hence there is little or no distortion. Unfortunately, empirical testing of the virtues of solidarity is extremely difficult.

5.3.3 POLITICAL SUPPORT

Another implication of these alternative welfare state regimes is the political support each of them is capable of attracting. There is a long-standing debate in Europe, as well as in the United States, regarding the relative advantages of alternative types of social policies. In the United States the debate focuses on the opposition between means-tested and universalistic programs, whereas in Europe it focuses on the opposition between a flat benefit and earnings-related benefit programs. Advocates of the universalistic program argue that programs that spread benefits widely garner greater political support than programs whose benefits go only to a minority of the population. On the other side, advocates of means-testing argue that universalistic programs are unnecessarily expensive for the purpose at hand: most of the subsidies go to the middle class and only a small proportion of the money reaches those who most need assistance. When contrasting flat-rate and earnings-related benefits systems, the same argument is used: the former costs less and is more effective at alleviating poverty; the latter attracts greater political support from the middle class that wants to get even.

Both sides of the debate can point to particular policies as supporting evidence. Advocates of categorical programs cite the popularity of social security in a number of countries. Advocates of means-testing counter it with the example of welfare programs, such as the RMI in France or the Minimex in Belgium, which are effective at alleviating poverty with few resources. In any case, over the last decade, elections have been won or lost because of the threat of social protection reforms. Some of these reforms, which were rejected by the voters, seemed to be fair from the usual equity–efficiency trade-off. This points to the

---

[5] See also Ooghe *et al.* (2003).

necessity for social scientists to move from the couple equity–efficiency to a *ménage à trois* with equity, efficiency and political sustainability.

In this debate one often finds the grass greener on the other side of the Channel. British economists tend to underline the pitfalls of a meager social protection based on means-tested or flat-rate benefits, whereas the Continental economists find their Bismarckian earnings-related programs expensive and inefficient. In that respect the recent evolution is quite interesting. EU governments tend to be less ideological and more pragmatic. For example, in Bismarckian countries where earnings-related benefits and employer/employee contributions are the 'official' doctrine, one progressively slides towards a system of flat-rate benefits and general tax revenue financing.

In a recent survey (Eurobarometer (2002)), Europeans were asked to choose between two options: a minimalist one suggesting the prospect of only basic social guarantees and increased individual initiatives, and a maximalist one calling for a continuous involvement of the State in a broad range of social protection benefits, even at the cost of increased taxes and benefits. The respondents' choices are reported in Table 5.3. Within the EU as a whole, the maximalist option is more widely supported than the minimalist

Table 5.3. A minimalist or a maximalist approach to social protection?

Country	Support for minimalism* (in %)		Support for maximalism** (in %)	
	1992	2002	1992	2002
Belgium	46	48	63	66
Denmark	54	54	58	59
France	41	44	65	67
Germany	27	31	59	62
Greece	37	42	76	86
Ireland	47	51	66	76
Italy	47	51	58	64
Luxembourg	27	30	66	71
Netherlands	50	53	53	58
Portugal	45	48	82	85
Spain	47	53	71	80
United Kingdom	44	47	79	83
EURO12	43	46	66	71

* Exact item: 'The government should provide everyone with only a limited number of essential benefits and encourage people to provide for themselves in other respects.'
** Exact item: 'The government must continue to provide everyone with a broad range of social security benefits even if it means increasing taxes and contributions.'

Sources: Eurobarometer (2002), Ferrera (1993)

one: 71 per cent versus 46 per cent. This would indicate that the status quo enjoys high public appreciation. By way of contrast, in the same survey a majority of Europeans expressed a preference for lighter taxes and contributions. Such a schizophrenic attitude is not at all surprising. People want more social protection without being willing to undertake further tax efforts to achieve it. Yet here as elsewhere, you cannot have your cake and eat it too. In our view, the alternative facing social protection does not lie between a maximalist and a minimalist option, the former being financially unfeasible. The real alternative is between guaranteeing a uniform but sufficient amount of benefits to the unemployed, the old, the sick, the disabled and the poor, as well as keeping the current system subject to a continuous erosion that will very likely lead to more pockets of poverty.

Another surprising observation comes from comparing the Eurobarometer outcomes in 1992 and 2002. The minimalist view gains little ground (from 43 to 46). By contrast, the maximalist view is winning (from 66 to 71) particularly in Greece, Ireland and Spain.

5.4 **Styles of welfare state**

Lately, a number of economists have considered a more pragmatic distinction, that between European and American-style welfare states. Their aim is to explain differences in redistributive policies between most European Union countries and the US. Instead of focusing on history and traditions, they base their explanation on the self-fulfilling role of agents' preferences, beliefs and their induced norms of behavior.

It seems widely accepted that redistribution is more easily supported if the focus is on bad luck rather than on individual responsibility or if it covers poverty driven by exogenous events rather than deprivation resulting mostly from laziness. It is sometimes asserted that Europeans put more weight (more probability) than Americans on random causes than on individual responsibility in order to explain poverty and deprivation.[6] Naturally, this conjecture cannot be tested empirically in an unambiguous way.

Benabou and Tirole (2002) use the concept of cognitive dissonance to explain individual belief in a just world. They show that, starting from the same initial conditions, society can evolve in two distinct directions and end up in two contrasting welfare states. The first is characterized by a high prevalence in the belief in a just world together with a relatively *laissez-faire* public policy. Both characteristics are mutually sustaining and generate an optimistic

---

[6] See Alesina and Angeletos (2002).

view of the world. The second welfare state is characterized by more real-istic pessimism and tends to be more generous, which in turn reduces the need for individuals to invest in positive beliefs. In this welfare state there is less stigma on the poor: one does not blame poverty on a lack of effort or will-power.

Bisin and Verdier (2004) focus on the interaction between redistribution policies and ethical beliefs, particularly the so-called 'work ethic.' Ethical beliefs are not given, but evolve over time, partially driven by parental edu-cation. Parents try to shape their children's beliefs according to their own beliefs. Redistribution is chosen through majority voting in a setting where the individual's work ethic is private information. The final solution, that is the long run redistribution equilibrium, may depend or not on the initial distribution of preferences. There are cases where multiple equilibria result from the same initial conditions, some with generous redistribution and some without.

Along the same lines, Lindbeck (1995a,b) analyzes the interaction between welfare state disincentives and the evolution of the work ethic.[7] There is also the work of Hassler *et al.* (2003) which leads to multiple equilibria of redis-tribution. They study a dynamic model with repeated voting: agents vote over distortionary income distribution, knowing that their votes will influence the next period vote. These models are theoretical. There are also papers that try to test differences in beliefs and norms between Europe and the US. Alesina *et al.* (2001), for example, present a study of the determinants of welfare state policies. They conclude that none of the economic, political and sociological factors they examine can explain the differences between the US and Europe. The explanation is to be found elsewhere. According to the *World Value Survey*, less than 40 per cent of Americans believe that luck determines income, while this percentage is close to 60 per cent for Italians, the Spanish, Germans and the French.

These are just a few representative samples of work aimed at explaining the emergence of two styles of welfare state, without resorting to what some economists consider as *ad hoc* assumptions: exogenous differences in values, traditions or preferences. One cannot but be ill at ease with some of these contributions, as behind a rigorous methodology they hide some value judge-ments. To start with, opposing the US (and generally the Anglo-Saxon world), to Europe (or Continental Europe), is a bit simplistic. Europe is very hetero-geneous. With characteristics such as social spending, unemployment rates, savings rates, age of retirement or education, it is difficult to find the US as an outlier. More seriously, this type of work tends to consider the US style as being the only sustainable welfare state.

---

[7] See also Lindbeck *et al.* (1999).

5.5 **The active versus passive welfare state**

Within Europe, one finds two contrasting views of the welfare state: a passive and an active view. The notion of active welfare state includes two ideas. On the one hand, there is the goal of a high employment rate and full responsibilization. On the other hand, there is the pervasive concern of offering protection to those who are excluded from the labor market. By default, a passive welfare state is one in which unemployment is viewed as a fatality and individual responsibility for being poor or unemployed is discounted.[8]

Admittedly this distinction is impressionistic. It appears in the opposition between two types of socialism: the socialism of Lionel Jospin[9] in France, and that of Tony Blair in the UK. It separates Europe with an East–West dividing line that goes through Belgium. Actually, the concept of activation divides Belgium between the Flemish North and the French-speaking South. In the North, policymakers speak of responsibilization in health care, compliance in unemployment insurance, workfare for the unemployed young without incurring negative reactions from the unions or from the political left. In the South these ideas are too often labelled as socially regressive. In that respect Belgium is an interesting real life laboratory. The two main regions have the same legal and fiscal institutions, and yet their view of the welfare state are quite opposite.[10] At the same time, Flanders has an unemployment rate of 7 per cent or half of what it is in the French-speaking region. Is this the cause or is it the consequence? Very likely both. In the activation approach, there is the idea that one has to fight both unemployment and poverty. As the US and the UK examples show, one can have quasi full employment as well as striking poverty.

Activation advocates argue that most schemes in traditional social protection do not encourage people to be active. Thus they should be abolished, or adapted in order to prevent the social safety net from becoming an 'inactivity trap.'[11] Moreover, the active welfare states should be proactive in preventing people from running into social aids (unemployment, disability, exclusion). There is the presupposition that individual vulnerability is at least in part socially determined and that intervention strategies are needed, for example, in the field

---

[8] See Vandenbroucke (2001), De Lathouwer (2004).

[9] Even though Jospin is for the time being retired from politics, his view is still that of the French Socialists and of a number of others in Southern Europe. See Chapter 14.

[10] As an example, the Belgian Minister of Employment Frank Vandenbroucke, one of the outspoken advocates of activation, recently introduced a reform allowing the federal agency that pays unemployment compensations to control the search efforts for employment of the unemployed. This reform was easily accepted in the north of the country, but fiercely rejected in the south by people who refuse this transformation of the federal agency into what they dubbed the 'National Office of Massive Exclusion.' Interestingly, acknowledging the difference in unemployment rates between the two regions, the Minister suggested that the controls ought to be less frequent where the rate of unemployment is the higher. This was considered discriminatory by some French-speaking political analysts.

[11] See Cantillon and van den Bosch (2002), Nolan and Marx (2000).

of training and education. The active welfare state intervenes on a tailor-made basis. Target groups and goals have to be identified carefully and programs must adjust to individual situations. Nothing should be taken for granted. There should be a constant questioning of whether the existing programs are appropriate to solving social problems, and not the other way around.

In almost all European countries, some types of activation have been installed in the welfare state with more, or less, success. Success depends in large part on the way reforms are presented. It is important to explain to the unions, the political left, and above all to the citizens, that an active welfare state is as protective as it is active. However, even with the best pedagogy, there will always be some resistance from some groups who stand to lose something in the process of reform.

A good example of activation is the Danish 'flexicurity' approach[12] which combines flexibility (a high degree of job mobility), social security (a generous system of unemployment benefits) and active labor market programs. Flexibility seems to work, at least, in Denmark where both unemployment and poverty are low. We come back to this in the chapter on unemployment. Compared to Belgium and France, Danish unemployment compensations are high, but after a short period there is the obligation to participate in activation programs.

5.6 **Alternative approaches**

The approach adopted in this book is pragmatic and purposely balanced. We consider that the priority should be given to the objectives of social protection: insurance against life uncertainty and poverty alleviation regardless of the institutions called for: the state, the market and the family. These are only viewed as alternative means to achieve these two objectives. In that respect, we are at odds with social philosophers and political scientists who tend to privilege one of these three institutions over the two other ones.

In this taxonomy of welfare state, Esping-Andersen (1990) distinguishes three views. First, there is the Anglo-Saxon view favoring individualism and markets, with the state and the family as nominal residual players. This view is associated with John Locke's tradition. Secondly, there is the Scandinavian view favoring the state along with the values of social democracy, universalism, egalitarianism and comprehensive social citizenship. This approach is in line with Jean-Jacques Rousseau's tradition. Here both the family and the market are extras.

---

[12] See OECD (2004d).

Finally, there is the Continental version involving France and Germany where the central locus is the firm viewed as a family and the southern countries where the family is the main player. In this view which is consistent with the philosophy of Thomas Hobbes, both the state and the market are residual players. The key concepts are those of corporatism and of solidarity within the firm and within the family.

We thus have several triptychs. On the left, one finds the state, the virtue of equality, Rousseau, the social democracy. In the center, one can see the family and the firm, the virtue of fraternity and solidarity, Hobbes and a corporatist society. On the right, there is the market, the virtues of freedom and liberty, Locke and a market economy. The approach chosen in this book is not to focus on just one of the panels of these triptychs, but on them all.[13]

5.7 Conclusion

In this chapter we have surveyed a number of taxonomies of social protection programs existing in the European Union. The main interest of these classifications is that different programs have different implications in terms of equity, efficiency and political sustainability.

We first focused on the characteristics of redistribution and generosity. We then introduced other features, such as the opposition between the active and the passive welfare state, or between two sources of social exclusion: bad luck or lack of responsibility. Finally we distinguished among three types of European welfare states based on their geography: Anglo-Saxon, Nordic and Continental.

[13] For an excellent discussion of these alternative views, see Masson (2004).

6 Social insurance and globalization

KEY CONCEPTS

OMC (Open Method of
    Coordination)
prisoner's dilemma
race to the bottom

social dumping
tax competition
yardstick competition

6.1 Introduction

Europeans are divided on two opposite approaches regarding globalization. The first one, which is dominant and named *pensée unique* (one track viewpoint) in France, consists in viewing economic integration with mixed feelings of hope and resignation. That is, hope that globalization will ensure steady growth and full employment for years ahead, and resignation regarding the diminishing role of national governments in economic and social policy. The second approach, epitomized by the Lisbon Group's Report (Petrella 1995), sees both globalization and competition as responsible for persistent unemployment, and implies the abdication of politics in favor of economics. This quite radical view presents the choice offered to European voters between the (German) social democratic model and the (American) capitalist model as equivalent to a choice between the plague and cholera.[1]

In this chapter we discuss two basic ideas. The first one is, that technological change as much as (if not more than) globalization leads to increasing income disparities; accordingly, European unemployment is caused by attempts at fighting these inequalities. The second one is that globalization, and specifically factor mobility, make it difficult for national governments to conduct any redistributive policy, thus leading to what is sometimes called 'the race to the bottom', or 'social dumping.'

---

[1] See on this Ravaillon (2003) and Agenor (2002).

6.2 **Benefits of globalization**

Over the past decade the economies of European countries have moved along two distinct tracks, neither of which has offered a compelling model for current public policy. The economies of Ireland and the United Kingdom, like those of North America and Australia, have been creating a lot of jobs, while suffering from wage stagnation and growing inequality. By contrast, economies in Continental Europe have featured growing wages and more modest income gaps, but have been far less successful at job generation. Must we simply decide between wage stagnation and double-digit unemployment? Or might there be a third way, one that combines jobs with decent compensation for workers, low poverty rates with employment? Arguably these are the fundamental questions facing all governments of the EU. We shall deal with them in Chapter 12. For the time being, let us look at the causes of these evolutions.

There is a tendency to blame unemployment or poverty on globalization: since growing trade with countries abundant in unskilled labor increases the premium on skill, this would explain inequality in North America and unemployment in Europe. This idea is attractive as it offers a broad common explanation for what is happening in the two sets of countries. Furthermore, it ties the labor market trends in advanced nations to the growth of international trade and the rise of newly industrialized countries. Finally, the idea of factor price equalization is well grounded in economic theory. As Krugman (1996) puts it: 'All in all, the proposition that globalization explains the simultaneous growth in inequality and unemployment makes a nice, intellectually appealing package; it is not surprising that it should command wide acceptance' (p. 21). Then Krugman bluntly adds: 'Unfortunately, empirical research is nearly unanimous in rejecting the idea that imports from the Third World have been a major factor in reducing the demand for less-skilled workers.' Indeed, one observes a consistent increase in the ratio of skilled to unskilled workers employed within each industry, despite the rise in the relative wage of the skilled. Thus one has to look elsewhere for the source of growing inequality and of rising unemployment.

It now appears to be widely accepted that the increase in the skill premium is primarily the result of technological change. The fact that both the relative wage and the employment of skilled workers have increased simultaneously indicates a change in the production functions that raises the marginal product of the skilled, relative to the unskilled. In countries such as the United States, and to some extent the UK and Ireland, where relative wages are highly flexible, the result is the growth of earnings inequality along with full employment. In European countries, where relative wages are rather fixed, one can only avoid such growth at the cost of unemployment. Furthermore, the effects of low-wage exports on employment are also negative (Krugman 1995) not because of the trade itself, but as a consequence of minimum wages. Also, a number of people have remarked that there is nothing new in the phenomenon of globalization. World markets achieved an impressive degree of integration during the second half of the nineteenth century. In 1970, for example, the United Kingdom and Germany were still below their 1913 trade levels. Maddison (1991) compares exports and GDP for 16 major industrialized countries: in 1913, exports were on average 21.2 per cent of GDP; in 1950, that figure had fallen to 15.1 per cent. It rose to 20.9 per cent in 1973 and to 24.1 per cent in 1987. There is evidence that the level of international trade engaged in by the major industrialized countries was not proportionately greater in 1994 than in 1914.

Long term comparisons show a trend towards regionalization rather than globalization of trade. For example, in 1953 the five more important European trading partners of Belgium and Luxembourg accounted for less than half of total imports and exports; in 1973, this share was approximately 70 per cent. What can we conclude from these figures? First, that globalization is not a new phenomenon. Secondly, that it cannot be considered as the main cause, or at least not the direct one, of increased unemployment. Thirdly, that it is largely responsible for the economic expansion of the last decades. However, there is a problem with economic integration particularly restricted to a regional area such as the EU: it raises the economic cost of redistributive policy, and thereby threatens a basic function of the welfare state.

6.3 **Tax competition and race to the bottom**

Even though economic integration is not responsible for increased income disparities, it is often argued that it imposes new constraints on the ability of governments to engage in income redistribution.[2] The potential mobility of factors of production, in response to differentials in taxation or benefits underlies traditional arguments for centralization of the redistributive functions of governments. Increased internationalization of factor markets implies that such a central government, that is, one whose geographical extent coincides with that of the relevant factor markets, does not have the power of a national government. There is thus a clear divorce between the political geographical coverage and the economic one. This is surely true of the EU particularly regarding the mobility of capital. The mobility of labor is still low compared, for example, to that within the USA; yet it represents quite a threat.

---

[2] For a survey of the literature see Cremer and Pestieau (2004), Cremer *et al.* (1997). See also Razin and Sadka (2005) who strongly believe that tax competition will eventually lead to the decline of the European welfare states. They argue that the US welfare state that is mainly organized at the federal level is more sustainable than the European ones.

Capital mobility explains why it is now impossible for European governments to effectively tax interest incomes. At best, these are subject to a withholding tax of 10 per cent that has to be contrasted with marginal rates above 50 per cent on labor income. This makes financing of the welfare state regressive and difficult, particularly in countries with a high outstanding debt. With labor mobility, the prognosis is even more pessimistic. As Sinn (1990) puts it, discussing European integration with increasing mobility, and no cooperation among governments, labor mobility could lead to 'the death of the insurance state.' He goes on: 'Any country that tries to establish an insurance state would be driven to bankruptcy because it would face emigration of the lucky who are supposed to give, and immigration of the unlucky who are supposed to receive. Voting with one's feet would only work if it could be limited to the young, and if the middle-aged managers and successful entrepreneurs could be prevented from migrating—a rather awkward idea. A Europe with competing tax systems and unrestricted migration would be like an insurance market, where the customers can select their company and pay the premium after they know whether or not a loss has occurred' (p. 502).

The perverse effect of governments competing for tax base was first underlined by George Stigler (1965) in an often quoted paper on the limits of local government. Indeed, one can view European governments as local governments lacking a central (supranational) authority. Stigler also noted that the current organization of local governments would make it impossible for any of them 'to obtain money from the rich to pay for the education of the children of the poor, except to the extent that the rich voluntarily assumed this burden' (p. 172).

To illustrate the issue at hand, we take the example of a small country whose national production results from the joint use of immobile capital and mobile unskilled labor. Figure 6.1 represents the marginal productivity of labor. In

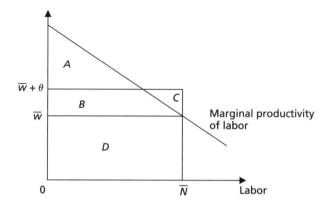

Figure 6.1. Race to the bottom

an autarchy the 'national' workers, $\bar{N}$, are paid their marginal productivity, $\bar{w}$. The wage bill is thus equal to area D, and aggregate capital income including profits is equal to area $A + B$.

There are few capital owners in this country, and they are willing (or forced) to devote part of their income to a redistributive transfer equal to θ. This implies that workers now receive a total amount of $B + C + D$ or $(B + C + D)/\bar{N}$ per unit. The capital owners now receive $A - C$. Suppose now that this economy is open to migration, and that the world wage rate is $\bar{w}$. This would have two consequences. First, as long as the offered wage is above $\bar{w}$, there would be some inflow of workers. Second, this inflow would only stop for $w = \bar{w}$ and thus $\theta = 0$. Without restriction to entry (which would be inefficient) or discriminatory treatment of newcomers (but this is ethically questionable), redistribution would be impossible.

Clearly, this is the extreme example of a small open economy that cannot retaliate. But even when a country can retaliate, redistribution will generally be lower than in an autarchy or in a cooperative setting. What is central to this phenomenon is the competition among national governments that leads them to reduce production costs, and hence social benefits. We here face quite a paradox: economic competition is generally deemed desirable, whereas political competition conveys inefficiency.

In order to illustrate this process of perverse competition and, more generally, the pitfalls of individualism, the economist uses a sort of fable known as 'the prisoner's dilemma.' This is the story of two people caught in possession of stolen goods. They are suspected of having stolen them, but there is no proof. Theft is punished by three years' imprisonment, while the simple possession of stolen property carries only a one-year sentence. The two people are questioned in separate rooms. Each can either deny having taken part in the crime, or admit to it, and in so doing implicate the other. If only one prisoner admits guilt, he is freed, and the authorities shift all the blame to the other prisoner, sentencing him to six years of imprisonment. If both prisoners deny all participation in the theft, they get only one year in prison. If they both admit, they are sentenced to three years prison. Table 6.1 shows the various possibilities of this 'game.'

The figures given represent the years in prison that prisoners A and B, respectively, would get for their choices. If each one could be sure that the other

Table 6.1. Prisoner's dilemma

	Prisoner B	
	Confess	Deny
Prisoner A		
Confess	3/3	0/6
Deny	6/0	1/1

Table 6.2. Tax game: capital income taxation

		Borduria	
		Do not tax	Tax
Syldavia	Do not tax	80/80	110/60
	Tax	60/110	100/100

one would say nothing, both would obtain the best solution for themselves. But, they will end up admitting their crime because they do not trust each other. Prisoner *A* tells himself that if he chooses to say nothing, his partner will not hesitate to betray him in order to escape prison, thus condemning him to six years' of imprisonment.

'The prisoner's dilemma' applies to a great variety of economic and political situations. It illustrates the cost of individualism and non-cooperation. It is a perfect description of the fiscal game in which the European nations are engaged, a game which tends to exempt capital income from taxation in order to attract it. By refusing to cooperate, each one ends up with a solution which is disadvantageous for everyone: zero taxation on that income and high taxation on other types of income. Table 6.2 illustrates this fiscal game in two countries: Borduria and Syldavia. The figures show the hypothetical level of well-being attained by each of these two countries in the four possible cases. The idea is simple: if one country taxes capital income heavily and the other hardly does so, it is to the full advantage of the latter where the capital will flow in. This country gets some tax revenue and benefit from a larger stock of capital for national production.

Note that if we consider two countries of different size, tax competition can improve the welfare of one of them. One thinks of Luxembourg, which clearly benefits from the inflow of capital from neighboring countries. One can, however, show that the gains of the smaller country are offset by the losses of the larger one.

6.4 **Some evidence**

As just shown, the race-to-the-bottom hypothesis appears reasonable, at least in theory. Yet up to now there is little supporting evidence at least.[3] Essayists usually cite anecdotes about firms moving from France to Scotland in order

---

[3] The recent history in the US is in that respect enlightening. At first sight the generosity of social policies of the states during the period 1994–2002, which is a period of devolution, has not changed. Yet

to benefit from better fiscal arrangements, or of executives leaving Paris for London where taxes are lower.[4]

One of the problems with this issue of supporting or non-supporting evidence is that there is no clear-cut way to test the reality of a race-to-the-bottom. We will use two types of evidence: one showing the effect of economic openness on the redistributive effort of national governments, and the other one looking at the change in the tax burden of capital (generally highly mobile) and labor (still not very mobile). A race-to-the-bottom would imply that international openness leads to less redistribution, and that the net taxation of labor increases relative to that of capital. As we shall see, the evidence for this is not conclusive.

In a recent study, Sorensen (2000) analyzes the evolution of average effective tax rates on labor and on capital from 1981–85 to 1991–95.[5] It appears that for the Northern countries, as well as Continental Europe, effective taxation on labor income has slightly increased (2.5%), whereas the effective taxation of capital has decreased even more slightly (1%). This shows that, in fact, governments try to shift some of the tax burdens towards the more immobile factors of production. Also during this period, the sharp drop in statutory tax rates on capital income suggests that governments are not insensitive to the threat of tax competition. However changes in effective rates are not very important, as seen in Table 6.3.

Table 6.3. Average effective tax rates on labor and capital income

	Total effective tax rate on labour income (%)		Effective tax rate on capital income (%)	
	1981–85	1991–95	1981–85	1991–95
Nordic countries				
Denmark	55.64	59.74	47.82	40.04
Finland	45.23	49.51	35.20	45.20
Norway	53.83	54.06	42.60	30.30
Sweden	57.44	59.80	47.40	53.10
Average	53.03	55.78	43.26	42.16
Continental Europe				
Austria	54.62	55.74	21.48	22.74
Belgium	52.90	54.71	39.50	36.00
France	52.53	56.98	28.40	24.80
Germany	47.07	50.23	31.00	26.50
Italy	43.75	52.76	25.30	34.50
Netherlands	57.25	59.84	29.70	31.90
Spain	37.71	40.92	13.90	20.30
Average	49.41	53.02	27.04	28.11

Source: Sorensen (2000)

looking at the content of their policies, one observes a retooling of programs with two consequences: increased interstate and intrastate inequality. See Meyers (2004).

[4] See Pestieau (2004).   [5] See also EC (1996).

Let us now turn to the evolution of income redistribution and poverty alleviation. Förster (2003) presents an excellent survey of the most recent work on this matter for the OECD.[6] His main conclusion is that in most countries redistribution keeps strong and that there is no clear tendency towards a race to the bottom. But this is not the only question. Another possibly more relevant question is whether or not there is a relation between openness and the variation in either the redistributive effort or in the performance of poverty alleviation. To measure openness we can use two indicators: the standard one, which is the ratio of exports plus imports divided by GDP and a more complex indicator that takes into account obstacles to international exchanges. They happen to be closely related; hence we only use the second one.

To measure the change in the effort of redistribution, we use three indicators. The first one is the variation in social expenditure which truly denotes the financial effort made by society. The second one is the variation in poverty alleviation measured by the reduction in poverty due to social transfers. The third one is the variation in the reduction of inequality measured by the difference between the Gini coefficient of income before and after transfers. We take the period 1985–95, which is a period of rapid economic integration and for which we have good poverty and inequality data for about 17 OECD countries. This data is presented in the appendix. In the majority of countries, efforts towards poverty alleviation and income redistribution have increased over the decade in question, which is already revealing. In other words, globalization has not lead to reduction in redistributive efforts for most countries. The only exceptions are Belgium, Ireland, Italy, and the Netherlands which experienced a reduction in their social expenditures. In Germany, the Netherlands and the UK, poverty alleviation has decreased. Finally, the reduction in inequality has been lowered in Germany and in the Netherlands. Note, however, that in these three cases the reduction is always very small.

To see if globalization plays some role, we now look at the effect of our indicators of openness on changes in social spending or in redistribution. We use simple cross-national regressions, represented in Figures 6.2–6.4. Clearly it appears that there is a negative relation between openness and both, the effort in redistribution (DPS) and the performance in redistribution (DRG), or poverty alleviation (DAP). Note that the relation between openness and change in social spending is not very good, unlike the one between openness and change in redistribution or poverty alleviation. This seems to indicate that openness influences the outcomes more than the means of redistribution; it could also mean that openness forces governments to make their social expenditure more contributory and less redistributive, or targeted to the poor.

---

[6] See also Atkinson *et al.* (1995) and Burniaux *et al.* (1998).

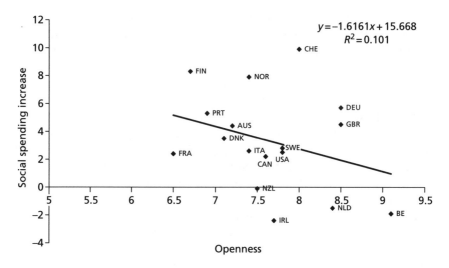

Figure 6.2. Social spending and openness

Source: See Appendix

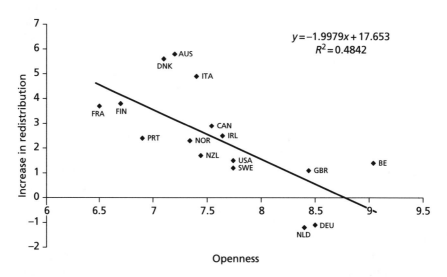

Figure 6.3. Redistribution and openness

Source: See Appendix

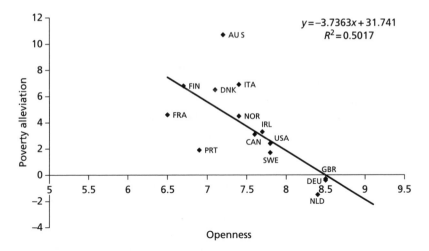

Figure 6.4. Poverty alleviation and openness

Source: See Appendix

6.5 **Why so little race to the bottom?**

A number of arguments have been advanced to explain why there is no drastic decline in redistribution even though labor, and above all capital, are free to move within the EU and even outside. The cost of mobility, as well as the uncertainty concerning tax-transfer policies in host countries, can prevent the race to the bottom. Let us consider other reasons. First of all, it might be too early to draw a conclusion. There are clear resistances to reforms aimed at dismantling the welfare state. Vested interests can prevent governments from down-sizing some redistributive programs. This is surely the case for public pension schemes. Not only are there lags in the behavior of governments, but also in the availability of data. In the previous section we looked at the 1985–95 decade. Data for the most recent decade is only available for a few countries, and does not allow for a conclusion one way or the other.

In addition, national governments can be insensitive to factor movements, in particular those known as 'brain drain.' Also national institutions are far from being transparent, which means that an effective fiscal wedge may not be perceived as such. Moreover, to the extent that benefits are linked to past contributions, or at least that entitlement is not automatic, welfare-induced migration should be limited. This raises an ethical issue. There seems to be a trade-off between the generosity of the welfare state and the political treatment of immigrants. A country adopting a policy of 'guest workers' can afford a more generous social protection than a country that right away awards all the benefits of social protection to an immigrant and his/her family. Even without resorting to a supranational government, one can expect a European government to reach multilateral agreements to the benefit of all parties concerned. What really matters is to have a population that truly supports redistribution. Indeed one sometimes has the feeling that European integration is just an excuse for fading out preferences towards redistribution. Finally, it is often argued that economic integration may sometimes reduce some of the need for national redistribution. In a world of uncertainty, factor mobility can in itself provide a form of market insurance against income risk. Access to external markets may limit factor price variation through spatial arbitrage, as well as obviate the need for social insurance (Wildasin 1995).

To sum up, we have seen that in an increasingly integrated world redistributive policies face the threat of a race to the bottom. But when looking at recent data, this threat does not seem to have been translated into reality: social redistributive policies are still alive and well. Yet, one is still left with the feeling that in the future the reasons just discussed will be less relevant, and that some race to the bottom will occur. The only way to reverse such an expected outcome is to rely on cooperation among national governments. In other words, the solution is to make supranational authorities responsible for redistributive policies. This is not out of reach, but it is up to the political will of each national government. Instead of waiting for the emergence of such a supranational government, a more pragmatic method has been recently proposed. It rests on the idea of governance by objectives and is called the Open Method of Coordination (OMC).

6.6 The Open Method of Coordination

Defining the OMC is not an easy task. It is a bit like the proverbial elephant: we may not be able to define an elephant, but we recognize one when we see one; if we don't have one to point to we use words like trunks, tusks, ivory, mammoth, ... The same holds with OMC. To define it we use words like benchmarks, yardsticks, best practises.

The OMC starts from the idea that each EU member state has its distinct history, and wants to run its welfare state its own way. Even though they face common challenges and risks, no country wants social uniformity, and all countries stand against additional transfer of national competencies to the EU, let alone harmonization for the sake of harmonization. The solution is in some kind of soft governance by objectives. It is here that the OMC that was coined at the Lisbon meeting in March 2000 makes its appearance. The OMC is a multistage process: first, member states define clear and mutually agreed upon objectives. Then on a regular basis, the best practises are identified for each one of these objectives. Hopefully each member country will then try to fill the gap between its own practise and the best practise for each of the objectives.

OMC is close to what is called 'political yardstick competition.' This surfaces when the performance of governments in various juridictions becomes sufficiently comparable so that the voters, after making meaningful comparisons between juridictions, can reward or sanction their own government.

The OMC involves fixing guidelines, establishing indicators and periodic monitoring. The commonly agreed upon indicators are of two kinds: the primary and the secondary. We focus on the primary which encompass financial poverty, income inequality, regional variation in employment rates, long term unemployed, joblessness, low educational qualification, low life expectancy and poor health. Table 6.4 gives the most recent available data for those indicators.

A number of questions come to mind. Why these particular indicators? Do some countries always come on top? Is it not naive to expect that comparing actual performance with best practise will be a sufficient discipline device,

Table 6.4. Structural indicators (2001)

Countries	Ineq	Pov	Ppov	Rpov	Reg	Drop	LTU	CUN	AUN	Life	Heath
Austria	3.5	12	7	19	2.6	10.2	0.9	4.1	7.9	78.6	4.33
Belgium	4	13	7	15	8	13.6	3.2	12.9	13.8	78.1	3.00
Denmark	3	10	6	13	–	8.8	0.8	–	–	77	12.00
Finland	3.5	11	6	17	8.9	10.3	2.5	–	–	78.1	4.33
France	4	15	9	19	6.4	13.5	3	9.2	10.3	79.3	2.60
Germany	3.6	11	6	19	6	12.5	3.8	8.9	9.7	78.5	1.69
Greece	5.7	20	14	28	4.6	16.5	5.4	5.4	9.2	78.1	6.50
Ireland	4.5	21	13	24	–	14.7	1.2	10.4	8.9	77.2	7.00
Italy	4.8	19	13	28	17.1	26.4	5.8	7	10.8	79.8	1.75
Luxembourg	3.8	12	9	17	–	18.1	0.6	3.4	6.7	78	–
Netherlands	3.8	11	5	20	2.3	15.3	0.7	6	6.9	78.3	2.33
Portugal	6.5	20	15	22	3.2	44.3	1.5	3.7	4.3	77	3.88
Spain	5.5	19	10	24	9.9	28.6	3.9	6.5	7.3	79.3	5.00
Sweden	3.4	9	–	17	4.2	10.5	1	–	–	79.9	3.67
United Kingdom	4.9	17	10	23	6.8	17.6	1.3	17	11.1	79.4	3.20

Source: Eurostat (2004)
Notes:
Ineq: Inequality of income distribution (income quintile share ratio)
Pov: At-risk-of-poverty rate after social transfers
Ppov: At-persistent-risk-of-poverty rate
Rpov: Relative median poverty gap
Reg: Dispersion of regional employment rates
Drop: Early school-leavers
LTU: Total long-term unemployment rate
CUN: Children aged 0–17 living in jobless households
AUN: People aged 18–59 living in jobless households
Life: Life expectancy at birth for men
Health: Self-defined health status by income level

Table 6.5. Average relative gaps (2001)

Countries	Ineq	Pov	Ppov	Rpov	Reg	Drop	LTU	CUN	AUN	Life	Health
Austria	0.14	0.25	0.20	0.40	0.02	0.04	0.06	0.05	0.38	0.45	0.26
Belgium	0.29	0.33	0.20	0.13	0.39	0.14	0.50	0.70	1.00	0.62	0.13
Denmark	0.00	0.08	0.10	0.00	–	0.00	0.04	–	–	1.00	1.00
Finland	0.14	0.17	0.10	0.27	0.45	0.04	0.37	–	–	0.62	0.26
France	0.29	0.50	0.40	0.40	0.28	0.13	0.46	0.43	0.63	0.21	0.09
Germany	0.17	0.17	0.10	0.40	0.25	0.10	0.62	0.40	0.57	0.48	0.00
Greece	0.77	0.92	0.90	1.00	0.16	0.22	0.92	0.15	0.52	0.62	0.47
Ireland	0.43	1.00	0.80	0.73	–	0.17	0.12	0.51	0.48	0.93	0.52
Italy	0.51	0.83	0.80	1.00	1.00	0.50	1.00	0.26	0.68	0.03	0.01
Luxembourg	0.23	0.25	0.40	0.27	–	0.26	0.00	0.00	0.25	0.66	–
Netherlands	0.23	0.17	0.00	0.47	0.00	0.18	0.02	0.19	0.27	0.55	0.06
Portugal	1.00	0.92	1.00	0.60	0.06	1.00	0.17	0.02	0.00	1.00	0.21
Spain	0.71	0.83	0.50	0.73	0.51	0.56	0.63	0.23	0.32	0.21	0.32
Sweden	0.11	0.00	–	0.27	0.13	0.05	0.08	–	–	0.00	0.19
United Kingdom	0.54	0.67	0.50	0.67	0.30	0.25	0.13	1.00	0.72	0.17	0.15

Source: Eurostat (2004)

particularly when the gap between the two is wide? Finally, is it possible to reduce the number of indicators to one or two?

The indicators given in Table 6.4 reflect different facets of exclusion. Yet looking at the correlations among them some appear to be redundant.

Indeed, if we define as redundant indicators those that have a correlation of more than 0.7, we can delete some of them. But in doing so we forgo what many would consider as the dominant factors of exclusion.

To make these indicators more comparable we have normalized them on Table 6.5, so that the minimum is 0 and the maximum is 1. Note that for life expectancy we have taken one minus the normalized life expectancy. It is thus tempting to add these normalized indicators in order to get a synthetic indicator of exclusion. This is given in Figure 6.5. In Figure 6.5 we also present the UN Human Development Indicator (HDI), which provides a qualitative measure of national welfare, and in which the level of income plays an important role. Yet there is some correlation between the two rankings.

It is clear that such a gross aggregation is questionable, particularly because it gives the same weight to all indicators. Another method consists of a softer technique of aggregation used to define best practise frontiers. With this multi-criteria method we do not obtain a full ordering of countries. A country is ahead of another one only if it dominates it for one indicator, and is not dominated by it for none of the others. Table 6.6 gives the ranking one thus obtains with the Data Envelopment Analysis (DEA) which truly envelops the data set and measures efficiency by the distance between actual achievement and this best practise frontier. It is clear that such a ranking is more politically acceptable than the one provided in Figure 6.5.

We look at four cases. The first two rank countries according to two sets of indicators: long term unemployment and inequality which seem to be the most

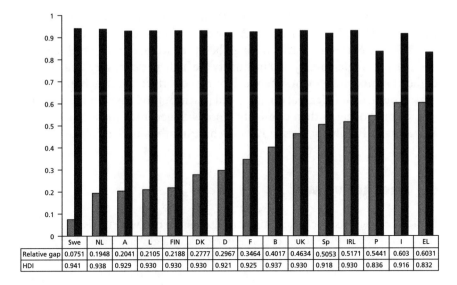

	Swe	NL	A	L	FIN	DK	D	F	B	UK	Sp	IRL	P	I	EL
Relative gap	0.0751	0.1948	0.2041	0.2105	0.2188	0.2777	0.2967	0.3464	0.4017	0.4634	0.5053	0.5171	0.5441	0.603	0.6031
HDI	0.941	0.938	0.929	0.930	0.930	0.930	0.921	0.925	0.937	0.930	0.918	0.930	0.836	0.916	0.832

Figure 6.5. Average relative gap

Table 6.6. Efficiency at nearing the best practise frontier

Countries	Without input		With social expenditure to GDP as input	
	Ineq LTU	Ineq LTU Drop Life Health	Ineq LTU	Ineq LTU Drop Life Health
Austria	1	1	0.563	0.664
Belgium	0.857	0.986	0.519	0.778
Denmark	1	1	0.563	0.566
Finland	1	1	0.563	0.770
France	0.857	0.998	0.467	0.700
Germany	0.857	1	0.467	0.758
Greece	0.571	0.983	0.467	0.606
Ireland	1	1	1	1
Italy	0.714	1	0.467	0.910
Netherlands	1	1	0.519	0.843
Portugal	1	1	0.609	0.837
Spain	0.714	0.993	0.583	0.875
United Kingdom	1	1	0.519	0.778

Source: Author's calculation

important, and then five indicators which are not correlated among themselves (LTU, Ineq, Drop, Life and Health). As the number of indicators increases from 2 to 5, the number of countries having a best practice goes from 7 to 9. The UK and Ireland, where poverty and inequality are high, perform very well because of their low unemployment. Then we look at the performance, taking spending into account. Countries that do not spend much, but still have good indicators, (e.g. Spain, Portugal) then dominate those with generous welfare states such as Denmark, Finland or Germany which have a rather high social burden.

6.7 Another view

Besides economists, social scientists are also concerned with the issue of globalization. They tend to focus on the emergence of a global capitalist empire in which national welfare states occupy a less central position than before. Sociologist Manuel Castells (2000), to take a well-known and typical example, argues that the modern state is facing a rapid decline. According to him, the planetary expansion of information networks is at odds with national state institutions and hierarchies: 'Networks dissolve centers, they disorganize hierarchy, and make materially impossible the exercise of hierarchical power without processing instructions in the network, according to the network's morphological rules. Thus, contemporary information networks of capital, production, trade, science, communication, human rights, and crime, bypass the national state, which, by and large, has stopped being a sovereign entity' (Castells 2000, p. 19). This view is questioned by Beland (2005), according to whom it seems to oversimplify the impact of economic and social globalization on state institutions and protection. 'Not passive victims of the globalization process, West European and North American policymakers have generally played the game of economic integration in order to gain electoral power and push for their own political agenda at home. Promising more prosperity as a consequence, these actors stress the fact that economic integration could benefit their country, and even stimulate welfare state development and coordination' (Beland 2005, p. 36). Now we do not deny that European integration has a number of positive implications for the population. The question that we want to raise in this chapter is that of the perenniality of social protection and redistributive policies.

6.8 Conclusion

In this chapter we have distinguished two levels of analysis of the alleged effect of globalization on income inequalities. The first level pertains to the distribution of earnings and income before taxation and transfers. The second one concerns the redistributive capacity of the welfare state. It would seem that technical progress is responsible for increasing wage disparities between skilled and unskilled workers, and that in that respect the role of globalization is overstated. However, globalization can explain why national governments find it more and more difficult to redistribute income. Indeed factor mobility leads to fiscal competition and social dumping in an economic union, without a central government to control for externalities induced by mobility.

APPENDIX

Countries	DAP	POV	DRG	GIN	DSE	OP1	OP2
AUS	10.7	9.3	5.8	30.5	4.4	0.40	7.2
BE	–	7.5	1.4	27.2	−1.9	1.37	9.1
CAN	3.1	10.3	2.9	31.1	2.2	0.72	7.6
DNK	6.5	3.8	5.6	22.5	3.5	0.66	7.1
FIN	6.8	4.9	3.8	26.1	8.3	0.66	6.7
FRA	4.6	7.5	3.7	27.3	2.4	0.43	6.5
DEU	−0.4	9.4	−1.1	27.7	5.7	0.48	8.5
IRL	3.3	11.0	2.5	30.4	−2.4	0.42	7.7
ITA	6.9	14.2	4.9	34.7	2.6	0.50	7.4
NLD	−1.5	6.3	−1.2	25.1	−1.5	1.10	8.4
NZL	–	–	1.7	33.7	−0.1	0.57	7.5
NOR	4.5	8.0	2.3	26.1	7.9	0.70	7.4
PRT	1.9	14.6	2.4	35.6	5.3	0.67	6.9
SWE	1.7	3.7	1.2	24.3	2.8	0.74	7.8
CHE	–	8.4	–	26.7	9.9	0.66	8.0
GBR	−0.3	10.9	1.1	32.6	4.5	0.58	8.5
USA	2.4	16.6	1.5	33.7	2.5	0.28	7.8
Period	1985–95	1995	1985–95	1995	1985–95	1995	1980–98

Definition and source of variables

OP1 Traditional index of openness measured as the ratio of imports plus exports divided by GDP.
Source: SIMA, The World Bank (2004)

OP2 CATO trade openness that measures the degree to which policies interfere with international exchange. It consists of 4 components: tariff rates, black market exchange premium, restriction on capital movement, actual size of the trade sector compared to the expected size.
Source: Gwartney and Lawson (2001)

DSE Variation in the share of public social expenditure in GDP.
Source: OECD (2001a), Social expenditure spending

POV The poverty rate measured with a poverty line equal to half the median income.
Source: Förster (2003)

DAP The increase in poverty alleviation, namely poverty with income before transfers minus poverty with income after transfers.

GIN The inequality index of GINI.
Source: Förster (2003)

DRG The increase in the reduction of inequality, namely GINI with income before transfers, minus GINI with income after transfers.

7 Welfare state and economic efficiency

KEY CONCEPTS

Consumer's surplus	distortionary tax
deadweight-loss	lump-sum tax

7.1 Introduction

European countries have experienced considerable improvements in well-being and standards of living over the past 50 years. This evolution includes widespread access to social protection benefits, a high degree of income redistribution, a reduction in absolute poverty and an increase in economic security for everyone. Such achievement can be attributed to the development of modern welfare states and to several decades of unprecedented economic growth. Yet, over the last decade, most EU economies have experienced declining growth and increasing unemployment. Economists, like most people have a short memory. They quickly forget the positive benefits brought about by the welfare state in terms of providing security and alleviating poverty and they blame its current state for slower growth. A number of economists now believe a retrenchment in social spending is necessary to revive economic efficiency and economic growth.

In this chapter, we shall discuss the arguments based on the disincentives embedded in the structure of the welfare state, and in its financing. In fact, most often the critique addressed to the welfare state can be extended to other forms of government spending. We shall also look at the aggregate evidence regarding the negative impact of the welfare state on the level or the growth rate of national income. The key issue is to figure out what we really want. Do we want the welfare state as it is, a market economy with no social protection, or a market economy with protection provided by the private sector? In other words, the issue of the counterfactual is crucial when discussing the dismantlement of the welfare state.

7.2 **Individual behavior**

Studies of individual behavior in the welfare state focus on the distortions that the welfare state carries with it. In these studies one looks at the effects of taxes and social insurance contributions, as well as at the effects arising from the expenditure side of the public budget: price subsidies, cash transfers and provisions of social goods like education or health care.

To illustrate these microeconomic effects, we first look at the effect of a wage tax on the welfare and the labor supply of workers. In Figure 7.1, Tintin's hours of work are plotted on the horizontal axis, and his hourly wage on the vertical. Tintin's compensated labor supply curve is labeled S_L: it shows the smallest wage that would be required to induce him to work each additional hour; or to put it otherwise, it gives the marginal disutility of providing one more hour of work. Initially, Tintin's wage is w and the associated hours of work L_1. For that amount of effort Tintin earns an income corresponding to the rectangle $0wdL_1$ for a disutility equal to the area $0adL_1$. His net gain (worker's surplus) is area adf.

Now assume that an income tax at a rate t is imposed. The after-tax wage is then $(1 - t)w$. What is Tintin's reaction going to be? It will depend on how he thinks that the tax proceeds are to be used. First, he can expect that the tax proceeds will be integrally returned to him; then he will still choose L_1. Thus he behaves as though he were seeing through the fiscal veil and recognizes the one-to-one relation between the taxes he pays and the benefits he receives.

Secondly, if Tintin does not acknowledge such a relation, even though he eventually gets back his tax payment (area $fihg$), he supplies L_2 hours. His

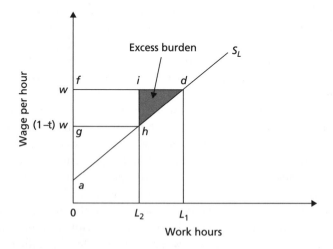

Figure 7.1. Excess burden of wage taxation

surplus after the tax is *agh*. The excess burden due to the tax-induced distortion is the amount by which Tintin's loss of welfare (*fdhg*) exceeds the tax collected. It is given by the triangular area *hid*. Quite often one approximates this excess burden, also called the deadweight loss triangle, by the formula:

$$1/2wLt^2\varepsilon,$$

where ε is the compensated elasticity of work with respect to the wage.[1] Note that when only part of the tax proceeds is given back because the rest is used for redistributive purposes, the loss to the worker consists of the deadweight loss and the amount transferred to other individuals. Yet, from an efficiency viewpoint, only the deadweight loss can be viewed as a real efficiency loss.

The importance of the excess burden of labor-specific taxes depends on three factors: the compensated elasticity of work, the linkage between taxes and benefits, and the perception of such a linkage. It has been argued (Summers *et al.* 1993) that the latter factor is related to labor market institutions. In 'corporatist' economies, wherein unions and management are in charge of wage and employment policy, taxes have a smaller distorting effect than they have in countries where individual workers make labor supply decisions. This argument is, in fact, used to explain why taxes tend to be high in these corporatist economies.

The effect of social protection on the incentive to work and on the efficiency of the economy can also be studied from the viewpoint of the beneficiaries. Unemployment or disability benefits and social security pensions would be truly non-distortionary if the probabilities of occurrence of the various states were exogenous. Yet, in reality, they can be influenced by the individuals' own actions. For example, the probability of unemployment is partly determined by the worker's choice of education and training, and by the intensity of his search for a new job, should he become unemployed. Social security can induce socially undesirable early retirement. Disability insurance can lead to more absenteeism on grounds of minor health complaints.

These work disincentives are increased when working implies high implicit or explicit marginal tax rates. This is the case of the poverty trap that results from the interaction between the tax and benefit systems. In some countries individuals in low paid jobs have little incentive to increase earned income since this could result in the withdrawal of benefits. At best, they are no worse off following an increase in labor supply and at worst, they are less well off. In this latter case, marginal effective tax rate or the benefit withdrawal rate is greater than 100 per cent.

So far, we have discussed the effects of the welfare state on labor supply. But it also has effects on savings behavior. Basically social protection may depress individual savings by taking the decision of whether to insure or to save against

---

[1] Recent calculations suggest a reasonable value for ε around 0.2.

risk out of the individual's hands. This critique is particularly addressed to pay-as-you-go social security which reduces private saving by guaranteeing retirees benefits financed by current workers. The effect of social protection in saving is a hot issue. However, the size of this effect is still debated.

From a review of the literature on the effects of the welfare state on labor supply and savings, we offer three remarks. First, most of this literature focuses on a fairly narrow range of questions that are studied because they lend themselves to feasible, empirical work. It fails to address the more fundamental and lasting effects of the welfare state on work and saving behavior. In that respect, Linbeck's (1995) point is worth mentioning when he discusses the possible feedback from social policies to preferences and behavior patterns. Accordingly, the challenge facing today's social protection is not only that the economic setting is totally different from that of the early fifties, but also that the individuals have tastes and political attitudes that may have fundamentally changed. This is very important. It means that rolling back social spending towards levels experienced in the fifties will not necessarily be accompanied by compensating responses from the private sector.

Second, by focusing on taxes and cash transfers one influences the conclusions drawn. Indeed, the provision of social goods, both private and public, could have a number of positive effects on the quality of the labor force. There exist several theoretical papers on endogenous growth that show that through health care and education the welfare state contribution to the stock of human capital can insure higher growth rates.

Third, the micro-textbook approach to the disincentive effects of the welfare state neglects a fundamental issue: what would society be without a welfare state? In order to pass judgement on the strengths and weaknesses of the welfare state, its redistributive and insurance functions, we have to take a closer look at the performance of private insurance markets and at the working of an economy with huge and unregulated income disparities (Sandmo 1995). In the following section (that may be skipped) we come back to the concept of excess burden.

7.3 A numerical example

Suppose that the consumer worker's preference for consumption and leisure is represented by a simple logarithmic utility function:

$$u(c, 1 - L) = \log c + \log(1 - L)$$

where c is the level of consumption or of disposable income and L is the labor supply. We see that both consumption and leisure $(1 - L)$ bring utility.

Suppose also that consumption is equal to $(1 - t)wL + T$ where t is the (constant) payroll tax rate, w, the wage rate and T, some benefits transferred back to the consumer. If t, w and T are given, maximizing $u(c, 1 - L)$, subject to the budget constraint brings a labor supply function and an indirect utility function that depends only on t, w, T:

$$L = \frac{w(1 - t) - T}{2w(1 - t)} \quad \text{and } v = 2\log[(w(1 - t) + T)] - 2\log 2 - \log[w(1 - t)].$$

We then distinguish among 4 cases:

Case 1: no taxation.

$$L_1 = 1/2 \quad \text{and} \quad v_1 = \log w - 2\log 2$$

Case 2: taxation according to the benefit principle (in other words, the consumer-worker knows at the outset that he will get back what he has paid for $(T = twL)$).

$$L_2 = 1/2 \quad \text{and} \quad v_2 = \log w - 2\log 2$$

Case 3: pure confiscatory taxation (the individual expects $T = 0$).

$$L_3 = 1/2 \quad \text{and} \quad v_3 = \log w(1 - t) - 2\log 2.$$

Case 4: distortionary taxation (the individual will ultimately get back his contribution but without seeing the direct link):

$$L_4 = \frac{1 - t}{2 - t} \quad \text{and} \quad v_4 = \log w - 2\log w - 2\log \frac{2 - t}{1 - t}.$$

One easily checks that for $t > 0$,

$$v_1 = v_2 > v_4 > v_3.$$
$$L_1 = L_2 = L_3 > L_4.$$

Furthermore, $v_4 - v_2$ is what economists call the deadweight loss, the efficiency cost, or the excess burden of taxation.

Finally, one could also consider the case of a confiscatory tax that would not be distortionary. This is also called a lump-sum tax. Instead of collecting twL through a tax on wage, the same amount would be collected without affecting the labor leisure choice.

Case 5: non distortionary confiscatory tax $(T = -tw/2)$

$$L_5 = 1/2 - t/4 \quad \text{and} \quad v_5 = \log w - 2\log 2 + 2\log(2 - t)/2$$

One sees that:

$$L_5 > L_3 \quad \text{and} \quad v_5 > v_3.$$

With a lump-sum tax as compared to a distortionary one, the utility loss is smaller and the labor supply is higher. It is important to note the difference between the excess burden of taxation and the income effect implied by a confiscatory (redistributive) tax. The first effect is a pure loss for the economy; it corresponds to a drop in GDP, whereas the second effect is only a loss if the tax proceeds are wasted. In the standard case where the tax proceeds are redistributed to people who need them because of poverty or accidental loss, these proceeds bring more social utility as these people are likely to have a higher marginal utility of income than the taxpayers. Those five cases are illustrated in Figure 7.2 for an arbitrary utility function.

Now, when turning to those receiving social protection benefits, one observes the same two effects: an income effect and a distortionary effect. There is no distortion (substitution) effect when the benefits are unconditional, or when they are given to categories that are perfectly observable. When using the same utility function one can distinguish among four cases.

We assume that the individual is not subject to the wage tax, but he may be subject to a means test. We also consider the possibility of an individual voluntarily stopping working, and who then receives an unemployment compensation or disability benefit.

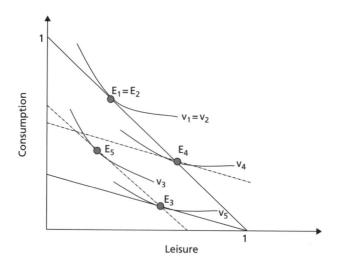

Figure 7.2. Disincentive for the workers

Case 6: Zero transfer

$$L_6 = 1/2 \quad \text{and} \quad v_6 = \log w - 2\log 2$$

Case 7: Transfer T without means test

$$L_7 = \frac{w - T}{2w} \quad \text{and} \quad v_7 = 2\log[w + T] - 2\log 2 - \log w$$

Case 8: Transfer T with means test

$$L_8 = \frac{w(1 - \tau) - T}{2w(1 - \tau)} \quad \text{and} \quad v_8 = 2\log[w(1 - \tau) + T] - 2\log 2 - \log[w(1 - \tau)]$$

Note that in the case where $\tau = 100\%$ corresponds to the so-called unemployment trap, one then has

$$L_8 = 0$$

Case 9: Discrete choice between working and receiving no benefit, or not working and receiving T

$$L_9 = 0 \quad \text{if} \quad \log T > \log w - 2\log 2$$

Those four cases are represented in Figure 7.3. One readily sees that both the income effect and the distortion contribute to less work.

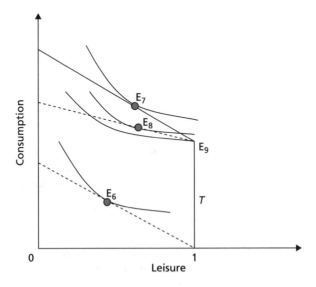

Figure 7.3. Disencentive for the beneficiaries

7.4 **Aggregate evidence**

An alternative approach to the study of the effect of social protection on economic performance is to test a macroeconomic relation. On the dependent variable side, one can look at the level of income or its growth rate. On the explanatory variable side, one can use either the level of social spending or the extent of income redistribution. At the outset there are two problems with such an approach. First, any aggregate relation of that kind is a black box: we have no indication as to the mechanism that is at work. Second, there is the causality issue. Why couldn't we hypothesize that a growing economy implies a strong demand for social protection and redistribution policies? In that respect, let us observe that, following Kuznets (1955), there have been a number of studies that conjecture that in advanced economies, growth results in a decreasing disparity in income.

Using the level of GDP or its growth rate leads to different predictions. Consider first the effect of social spending on the level of GDP. A cut in social spending induces a temporary rise in the growth rate; GDP rises to its new equilibrium level, but there is no permanent increase in the rate of growth. Alternatively, there is the alleged effect of the level of transfers on the long-run rate of growth. Accordingly, a reduction in the welfare state is predicted to raise the growth rate permanently. Using the data of Chapter 3, Figure 7.4 shows the relation between average GDP growth over the period 1980–98, and the social

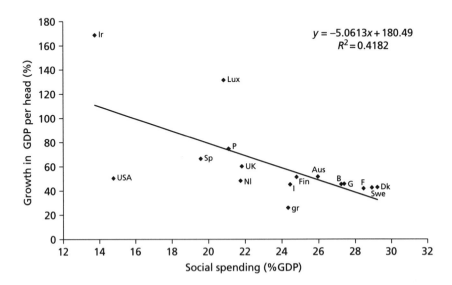

Figure 7.4. Social spending in 2001 and per capita GDP growth rate over 1980–2001

Sources: OECD (2004a), OECD (2004b)

burden in 1998. The estimated regression line is given by

$$\text{GDP growth} = 118 - 2.97 \text{ social burden} \quad R^2 = 0.32$$

There are also theoretical predictions as to the effect of inequality on economic growth. Two mechanisms have been suggested by which redistributive policies could reduce aggregate growth. Post-Keynesian economists (Kaldor 1956) argue that since a high level of savings is a prerequisite of rapid growth and the marginal propensity to save increases with income, policies that redistribute income from the rich to the poor reduce saving and thereby growth. There is also the political economy argument (Persson and Tabellini 1994) that an initially unequal distribution of market income leads to political pressures for redistributive policies that distort economic incentives and thereby reduce growth. Thus, *ex ante* inequalities are ultimately bad for growth since they engender policies that are themselves bad for growth.

In these macroeconomic studies one finds the same problem as in the microeconomics ones. The welfare state and redistributive policies can also have a number of positive effects. Indeed it is clear that the welfare state can stimulate growth by a variety of ways by improving the quality of human capital, increasing social cohesion, easing the credit constraints and fostering risk taking. One thus needs to look at the empirical evidence.

Atkinson (2000) presents recent studies on the effect of social protection on growth; these studies use a variety of methods to overcome the usual econometric problems, including those of causality. Out of the ten studies listed, two find an insignificant effect of welfare state spending on annual growth rates; four find that social transfers are negatively associated with average growth; and another four find a positive relation between the welfare state and growth.

What can we conclude from the macroeconomic studies of the effect of welfare state spending on economic performance? There are three levels of answers. First, there is the answer of the laymen who are also voters. Basically, they would like to keep the benefits of the welfare state but pay a lesser price. Secondly, there is the empirical evidence which at this moment cannot provide a reliable guide to the likely implications of cutting welfare state spending. Thirdly, there is the theoretical understanding of the relation between the welfare state and economic performance which is still in need of further investigation.

A recurrent issue in development economics is the relation among three concepts: poverty, inequality and growth with questions such as: is growth pro poor? Is inequality bad for growth? Can growth lead to less poverty but more inequality? There exist a huge number of articles and books, more empirical than theoretical, more positive than normative, on the effect of poverty or inequality on growth, and of growth on inequality or poverty.[2] Even though

---

[2] See, e.g. three books on that subject published by the United Nations Institute (World Institute for Development of Economic Research) WIDER in 2004.

most of the discussion concerns less advanced countries, that is, countries without a sensible welfare state, it has some bearing on the theme of this chapter. In the ongoing debate, the poverty measure is absolute (e.g. equal to $1 a day), and the conventional wisdom is that growth reduces poverty, given that income inequality does not increase. Furthermore, high levels of inequality can depress the rate of growth because of its undesirable political and social impacts on crisis, political stability and education. In other words, reducing inequality is good for growth and for poverty alleviation. Unfortunately, since the early mid-1980s, inequality has risen in most less developed countries, and in many cases sharply.

7.5 **An historical view**

While most of the debates over the efficiency of the welfare states deal with recent decades, it must be noted that Europe's welfare states are much older than that. In a provocative and challenging book, Peter Lindert (2004) offers a monumental history of two centuries of social spending, and he concludes that the big European welfare states—which are undoubtedly expensive—are surprisingly efficient. But, at the same time, they are less redistributive than one might expect. This conclusion surely goes against Ricardo's conjecture that Europe's redistribution would lead to the 'plague of universal poverty.'

Let us follow Lindert's main argument that deals with the efficiency of the welfare state, and particularly, of its financing. Compared with Americans, Europeans place far more of their tax burden on consumption than on income, thus doing less damage to the incentive to save and to work. Furthermore, also unlike the Americans, when they tax income they lean on labor rather that on capital. One knows that it is easier to discourage capitalists from investing than workers from laboring. Even today, Europeans treat capital better than earnings. This appears clearly in Table 6.3 (p. 56). Note that as far as incentives are concerned, the marginal tax rates are those that matter, and the gap between marginal rates of capital income taxation in Europe (0 per cent in Sweden) and in the US (46 per cent) is quite astonishing.

Let us now look at the other side of Lindert's conclusion: this structure of taxation is efficient but wholly inequitable. It is known that capital owners, who tend to be richer, get off lightly while labor carries a heavier burden because of lower disposable income and higher unemployment. Lindert's conclusion is interesting for two reasons: it covers two centuries and goes against the tide. It also needs to be qualified in a number of aspects. First the European and American tax systems have evolved and converge somehow. In addition the efficiency of the tax system is just a part of the efficiency of an economic system. On the redistributive side, one realizes today that little redistribution is achieved through the tax system. Most of the redistribution is effected by social insurance (health and pensions) and by public spending (education).

7.6 **Conclusion**

At the end of this chapter one is left with very mixed impressions. The question we started with was whether or not the welfare state was responsible for the decline in economic performance. At the micro level, social protection brings distortion in the choices of contributors and of beneficiaries. Yet, the empirical evidence indicates that the cost of these distortions is rather limited. At the macro level, one cannot infer much from a negative relation between the social burden and GDP growth. If there is any relation between these two variables, it is the result of a very intricate model that appears to be a black box.

Having said this three conclusions emerge. First, the welfare state is likely to have modified the preferences of individuals. By overprotecting certain categories of people, and, not necessarily the neediest, it leads to a loss in the spirit of responsibility and initiative. The second conclusion is that the decline in economic growth and pressured public finance—regardless of whether or not its cause is the development of the welfare state—calls for its partial retrenchment. Finally, most of the work on the effect of the welfare state on growth and unemployment deals with a relatively short and recent period. A longer run view might be useful.

8 Efficiency of the welfare state

KEY CONCEPTS

Best practice frontier   productive efficiency
Matthew effect

8.1 Introduction

In general, when one considers the concept of efficiency coupled with the welfare state, one immediately thinks of the effects on the efficiency of the economy of the welfare state, notably the taxes implied and the benefits generated. This question has been widely discussed in recent works.[1] One of the main charges addressed to modern welfare states is that they impair economic performance and international competitiveness. It was the topic of Chapter 7. Another charge, just as widespread, is their inefficiency in providing social services, and their responsibility for the proliferation of costly transfer programs that miss their target populations. This second charge is thus different from the first one, although not totally unrelated. It concerns the economic efficiency of the welfare state *per se*, and it is the topic of this chapter.

Each type of social expenditure has what could be called a target population, which it reaches via a more or less lengthy process. To take an example, the fact that 100 million Euros are devoted to social housing does not mean that the natural beneficiaries of this type of program, namely needy households, will receive a service equivalent to that amount. At each stage of the process that provides such a service dysfunctionings may appear, with the consequence that the amount initially intended for this service is greatly reduced. At the production stage corporatism, self-interest and mere incompetence can lead to the first failures in functioning. Further down the line, at the allocation stage, the benefits, if any, may be attributed to population groups that do not really need them, while neglecting those for whom they could be vital. This is another type of failure.

---

[1] For a survey, see Atkinson (1995). See also the work of Lindbeck (1995a,b).

We have just mentioned two forms of failures in functioning, 'productive inefficiency' and 'distributive inefficiency.' The first has been widely studied by production economists, and it applies to components of the welfare state that involve the production of services. This is the case of hospitals, schools, day-care centers where services (outputs) are produced out of some human and material resources (inputs). The second has been studied particularly by economists and sociologists, and concerns income transfers programs, particularly means-tested ones. Note, however, that agencies in charge of these transfer programs, for example, the social security administration, can also be inefficient if they require excessive administrative costs.

In this chapter we will discuss those types of inefficiency with a particular focus on productive inefficiency. We will present a methodology that is not often applied to the welfare state: the efficiency frontier approach.[2] Also, we will report some published and unpublished results. Our main purpose is to show that one can measure inefficiency in the welfare state, not just talk about it in abstract terms, as is often the case. In so doing, we want to address a number of policy questions. When inefficiency is detected, can it be corrected? Can it be explained? Is it inherent to the public sector? In other words, would privatizing some of the activities of the welfare state wherever possible increase their efficiency? Our motivation comes from a conviction that removing these efficiency slacks could alleviate part of the financial strains that burden most welfare states. Too often we hear unqualified statements as to the inefficiency of government action. These, in turn, can be used to justify hasty dismantlement or privatization of a specific program or service. We believe that the welfare state, like any accused, is entitled to a due process and particularly to a fair trial. If then its inefficiency is proved without extenuating evidence, then measures of rolling back or of privatizing can be taken.

The rest of the chapter is organized as follows. The next section is devoted to distributive inefficiency that arises in the allocation of social transfers or services. Section 8.3 deals with the administrative cost of transfer and social insurance programs. Section 8.4 introduces the efficiency frontier approach. This approach can be applied to a number of specific social services (section 8.5) or to the whole welfare state (section 8.6). The final section discusses the causes of inefficiency in social spending and presents a few recommendations.

8.2 The Matthew effect

One can speak of distributive inefficiency of social policy when the programs implemented do not help to remove the insecurity of existence from

---

[2] Already mentioned in Chapter 6 about the OMC.

beneficiary households or individuals, despite sufficient resources to achieve this objective. How can this phenomenon be explained? Simply by the fact that needy households do not exercise their right to benefit from these social protection programs, while other households not suffering from precarious conditions do benefit from them. Furthermore, this inefficiency is not limited to social protection in the strict sense of the term, but also to a number of social facilities and services: study grants, social housing, social assistance, and so on. This phenomenon of unequal and inappropriate distribution of the state's social expenditure has been studied under the name of the 'Matthew effect.'[3] For cultural and institutional reasons, well-off social groups often benefit from social provisions intended for disadvantaged groups. These are stopped by administrative complexity and by fear of stigmatization. Admittedly, the Matthew effect does not explain everything; some new types of poverty and exclusion are not being provided for in the existing social assistance programs.

The Matthew effect has been widely studied in a number of European countries, including Belgium (Deleeck (1979)) and the UK (Le Grand (1982)) in the 1970s and 1980s. It has received less attention over the last decade.[4] This might reflect the fact that today very few people believe that expenditure in social services benefits primarily the less well off. It came as a surprise when Peter Townsend (1979) concluded his survey on poverty in the UK: 'Contrary to common belief, fewer individuals in households with low rather than with high incomes receive social services in kind of substantial value' (p. 222). Today, most social scientists admit that social spending in areas such as education, health, transport, housing, is distributed in favor of the higher social groups.

As Le Grand (1982) puts it, there are different kinds of equality pertaining to social services: equality of public expenditure, equality of final income, equality of use, equality of cost and equality of outcome. He then studies whether public spending on health care, education, housing and transport promotes equality in any of its interpretations. Focusing on equality of public expenditure in Britain, he shows that the top socio-economic group receives up to 40 per cent more national health service expenditure per sick person than the bottom group, accounting for difference in age and sex. The top fifth of the income distribution receives nearly three times as much public expenditure in education per household as the poorest fifth. Public expenditure on housing

[3] The concept of 'Matthew effect' is widely used by sociologists in different areas. It is called after the 'Parable of Talents' as told in the Gospel according to Matthew: 'For to everyone that has, more will be given, and he will have abundance; but from him who does not have, even what he has will be taken away' (Matthew 25–29). Recently Paul Krugman (New York Times, June 1, 2004) has introduced the concept of Dooh Nibor Economics (Robin Hood in reverse) to characterize large scale transfer of income from the middle class to the very affluent.

[4] At least in developed countries. In the less advanced countries, this issue has been widely studied by the World Bank with the famous concept of 'programs for the poor are poor programs.'

favors the better off, with the highest group receiving nearly twice as much as the lowest. Finally, the richest fifth of the income distribution receives about ten times as much subsidy per household on rail travel, and seventeen times as much on private transport as the poorest fifth.

As another example of the Matthew effect, one can mention the use of subsidized child care in Belgium. In 1992, 28.2 per cent of households with children under three used that facility, with a wide dispersion across classes of disposable of income. The rate of participation was of 15.5 per cent for the bottom decile, 21.8 per cent for the fifth decile and 47.8 per cent for the top decile. This rather regressive effect still holds even after controlling for working mothers.[5]

This evidence can readily be applied to other countries with strong social policy. However, it calls for two caveats. First, as has often been noted, the political survival of the welfare state might require that not only the poor benefit from social policy, but also the middle class. In other words, without the Matthew effect there could be no social program at all. Second, one has to keep in mind that, fortunately, the Matthew effect does not apply to the entirety of the welfare state. There are many redistributive programs that work, which explains the relatively good performance of the welfare state at fighting poverty and social inequalities.

8.3 **Administrative costs**

In welfare and social insurance programs, the productive activity is limited to one of financial intermediation. The question raised is that of the relative administrative costs associated with public and private intermediation. This has been particularly studied in the field of retirement and health care insurance for which there exist a number of empirical studies (Mitchell 1997). The current evidence pertains to international cost comparison of social insurance and cost comparison between private and social insurance.

The administrative costs of social insurance vary greatly across countries and institutional settings. Table 8.1 reveals that countries in the European Union spend about 3.5 per cent of their annual budgets on social security in administrative costs. This ranges from a low 1.22 per cent in Austria to 6.72 per cent in Greece. Part of the explanation for these marked cost differences is that social security systems vary across countries in terms of the particular mix of social assistance and insurance, and in terms of the types of payments offered. Another part of the explanation lies in the economies of scale. It appears, from a multivariate comparison of social security costs in a sample

---

[5] See Storms (1995).

Table 8.1. Administrative costs as a percentage of social security benefit expenditures in the European Union and the USA

Austria	1.22	Italy	2.20
Belgium	4.55	Luxembourg	2.74
Denmark	2.98	Netherlands	3.10
Finland	3.96	Portugal	4.86
France	4.18	Spain	2.81
Germany	2.86	Sweden	4.24
Greece	6.72	UK	3.10
Ireland	4.88	USA	3.28

Source: Mitchell *et al.* (1994)

of countries, that a one percent increase in participation raises costs by only 0.6–0.9 per cent. The same study shows that a universal demogrant system is significantly less costly to administer than a means-tested or an earnings-related program (Mitchell 1997).

A comparison of publicly managed insurance systems with privately managed alternatives indicates that, in general, the latter is considerably more costly. In the US it is estimated that roughly 12 per cent of the revenue of the health insurance industry goes for administrative expenses. This percentage is well above the cost of state-managed health insurance in European countries, and even in the US. As noted by Diamond (1992), this high percentage is primarily a reflection of returns to scale in transactions including advertising and commissions. In part it is also due to adverse selection because of the need to underwrite in details. Finally, it can be attributed to the high turnover that characterizes private health insurance. The same cost difference is observed in retirement insurance. For example, it is now clear that the new Chilean private pension system that many consider as a model is very expensive, a lot more expensive than well-run, unified, government-managed social security systems (Valdes-Prieto 1998 and Gill *et al.* 2004). The life insurance industry has costs that run 12–14 of annual benefits, while social security administration reports costs at less than 1 percent.

It is important to recognize those cost differences. Too many people think of privatization as a route to greater efficiency and lower costs. Yet as early as 1942, Beveridge (1942) referred to a 'markedly lower cost of administration in most forms of state insurance.' In defence of private insurance, a number of observers note that it is likely to offer better and more diverse services in exchange for these higher costs. There would be a trade-off between diversity and transaction costs that requires further study.

So far, the focus is on the efficiency of social insurance programs and their administrative costs. In this particular activity the index of performance is unidimensional; thus measuring the efficiency of insurance programs is quite easy. The difficulty arises when there are several kinds of services produced or provided, and resources used. We now turn to this problem.

8.4 Doing better with less

For an economist an activity is called productively inefficient if the same production of goods and services can be carried out with fewer resources, or if more can be produced with the resources used. To illustrate this concept a figure may be helpful. Being restricted to two dimensions, we consider an activity a that produces a service y_a out of an input z_a. Figure 8.1 represents such an outcome, as well as a curve that represents the productive efficiency frontier. This curve is the yardstick with respect to which the efficiency of a can be assessed. The relative vertical distance between a and this frontier measures what we call the productive inefficiency of a. Note that such a measure can apply to a setting with multiple outputs and inputs, possibly including quality indicators.

The measuring of productive efficiency would be a rather simple exercise if the efficiency frontier were known. Unfortunately this is not the case as the true frontier cannot be found in the blueprints of a social engineer. It must thus be inferred from the reality; that is, constructed from a sample of possibly inefficient observations. The dots on Figure 8.1 represent such a sample.

There are different types of methods that vary from the estimation of a prespecified production function to the construction of a stair-shaped envelope of the input–output points (Free Disposable Hull, FDH). Whatever the method chosen, parametric or not, stochastic or deterministic, one should realize that

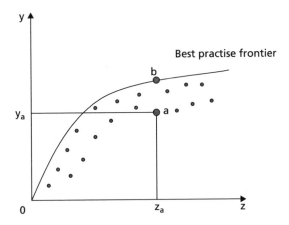

Figure 8.1. Productive inefficiency

the productive inefficiency so measured is, of course, a relative one. Hence, one often uses the term 'best practice' frontier. This frontier is made up of those observations that appear to be the best ones in the sense of some posited assumption of dominance.

For that reason the choice of the sample of observations is crucial. It is important that they originate from similar conditions as to the technology. To take the case of a cross-section sample of retirement homes, the question of spatial homogeneity is quite relevant. It is not impossible that geographical or institutional differences go a long way towards explaining variations in performance. Part of the efficiency assessment exercise consists in accounting for these differences.

One can see right away the limitations of the efficiency frontier approach for the purpose at hand. First, it only applies to components of the welfare state in which there is production of services: hospitals, social security administration, social work. Secondly, since the method is comparative, it concerns activities with a large number of comparable productive units. Note, however, that in certain instances intertemporal or international comparisons can enlarge the sample of activities whose performance is to be assessed. As it appears clearly from Figure 8.1, productive inefficiency measures waste of resources. Why produce only a when b is attainable?

It is clear that productive efficiency should not be the sole objective of social policy makers. There are other objectives for sure: first of all, achieving some redistribution as we have seen, but also fostering employment and growth while keeping within the financial constraints. Some of these objectives are not always compatible. Productive efficiency is, indeed, the only objective whose achievement does not impede the achievement of the other objectives. Producing too few services or employing too many resources, as compared to what is technically feasible, cannot be justified in terms of any of the other objectives traditionally assigned to the welfare state.

8.5 Survey of productive efficiency studies

For a long time there was nothing but anecdotal evidence to document the efficiency of the welfare state. Fortunately, over the last decade, there have been a number of studies that have used the productive efficiency approach to measure the efficiency of various sectors of the welfare state. Going back to Figure 8.1, the procedure is quite standard. We collect data on a sample of activities that can be represented by dots. Then we construct a frontier that essentially envelops that data. For each observation, for example, a, one calculates its degree of productive efficiency or the ratio az_a/bz_a. This ratio

Table 8.2. Survey of a number of productive efficiency studies

Areas	Production unit	Studies	Country	Productive efficiency (in %)
Health	Hospitals	Bosmans/Fecher (1999)	Belgium	54 to 78
		Dervaux et al. (1994)	France	75
		Burges/Wilson (1993)	USA	85
		Holvad/Hougard (1993)	Denmark	68 to 78
		Grosskopf et al. (2001)	USA	76 to 94
		Morrison-Paul (2002)	Australia	73
Social	Day care	Bjurek et al. (1992)	Sweden	89
	Retirement homes	Boveroux et al. (1995)	Belgium	93 to 96
		Sexton et al. (1989)	USA	69 to 79
		Kooreman (1994, 1995)	Netherlands	80 to 94
Education	High schools	Wyckoff/Lavigne (1991)	USA	81 to 86
		Mancebon and Bandrés (1999)	Spain	91
	School districts	Banker et al. (2004)	USA	71
		Grosskopf et al. (1997)	USA	71
	Universities	Abott and Doucouliagos (2003)	Australia	94 to 96
		Ng and Li (2000)	China	65 to 67
Community	County council	Salinas et al. (2004)	UK	97
	Municipalities	Erlandsen and Forsund (2002)	Norway	76 to 93

would be equal to one, if the observation were lying on the frontier. The last stage attempts to explain, when possible, some of the observed efficiency slacks.

Table 8.2 provides a number of results obtained recently. These concern four areas of social spending: health, education, day care and retirement homes.

These studies reported in Table 8.2, as well as a number of others (Pestieau and Tulkens 1993, Gathon and Pestieau 1996), lead to three conclusions: (i) there are serious productive inefficiencies; in other words, more and better could be done with less; (ii) these inefficiencies are not specific to a particular type of organization (non-profit, state-owned, for-profit); (iii) competition, autonomy and flexibility could help to reduce a substantial proportion of these inefficiencies.

For a long time there was a strong belief among economists that public sector managers, unlike their private sector counterparts, do not have to worry about losses, or become the victims of takeovers. Hence, they have little incentive to carefully monitor the activities of their enterprises or services. But it is now widely accepted that the productive efficiency of a public or private activity depends on both the market environment and the institutional setting in which it operates. A privately owned monopoly or a regulated firm may produce very inefficient results, while a publicly owned operation that is subject to a lot of competition and few legal restrictions may produce quite efficiently. This is a theoretical statement backed up by a number of empirical studies. It implies that, to enhance efficiency in the welfare state, it is important that it opens its operation to competition, and if necessary, that it allows private companies to compete along with public ones for contracts to supply particular services.

This conclusion is somehow at odds with the one reached on financial intermediation where being a single provider was cost efficient. The reason for this contradiction lies in the underlying technology. Activities such as day care centers or retirement homes quickly reach their optimal scale; in other words, multiplying them is scale efficient and allows for some form of competition. On the other hand, in activities such as social security or unemployment insurance, fixed administrative costs can be spread over a large group of people, and their scale economies dominate the potential gains arising from competition.

8.6 **Public spending efficiency**

Public expenditures for education and health are considered the most efficient means of redistribution in today's welfare states. The previous section presented some results concerning their productive efficiency at the 'firms' level.

Afonso and St Aubyn (2004)[6] have studied the same question in an international setting. For education they use the PISA indicator[7] as output, plus the number of hours per year spent in school and the number of teachers per student. The results of their efficiency analysis, based on a non-parametric method (Free Disposable Hull) are presented in Table 8.3. Focusing on the EU15, we see that Belgium, which is known for its high ratio of teachers to students in secondary education is ranked last. By contrast Sweden and Finland, which have a high score on the PISA scale are first.

For health care, Afonso and St Aubyn use the Data Envelopment Analysis (DEA) with three inputs: the number of doctors, nurses and hospital beds and two output indicators: infant mortality and life expectancy. The efficient EU countries are Spain, Sweden and the UK. Those badly ranked are the Netherlands, Germany and Austria, which is a bit surprising. This ranking is more questionable than the previous one, not because of the method, but because of the choice of inputs that reflect qualitative aspects one would expect to find on the output side.

8.7 **An aggregate view at efficiency**

The modern welfare state encompasses a variety of activities ranging from pure financial intermediation, such as social security, to the production of

[6] See also Afonso (2004), Afonso *et al.* (2003) and for health care, Osterkamp (2004).

[7] PISA stands for Program for International Student Assessment. It is a survey of 15-year-olds in most OECD countries that assesses their skills and knowledge.

Table 8.3. Health and education efficiency scores, 2000

Country	Input* efficiency score	Country	Input** efficiency score
Australia	*0.832*	*Australia*	*0.850*
Austria	0.703	Belgium	0.689
Canada	*1.000*	*Czek Republic*	*0.931*
Czek Republic	0.681	Denmark	0.912
Denmark	0.808	Finland	1.000
Finland	0.806	France	0.832
France	0.835	Germany	0.961
Germany	0.604	Greece	0.758
Greece	0.820	*Hungary*	*0.801*
Hungary	*0.480*	Italy	0.730
Ireland	0.716	*Japan*	*1.000*
Italy	0.798	*Korea*	*1.000*
Japan	*1.000*	*Mexico*	*1.000*
Korea	*1.000*	*New Zealand*	*0.914*
Luxembourg	0.707	Portugal	0.879
Mexico	*1.000*	Spain	0.876
Netherlands	0.579	Sweden	1.000
New Zealand	*0.830*	UK	0.922
Norway	*0.726*		
Poland	*0.679*		
Portugal	0.844		
Spain	1.000		
Sweden	1.000		
Turkey	*1.000*		
UK	1.000		
US	*0.725*		
Average	0.814		0.892

*DEA analysis, 3 inputs (doctors, nurses and beds) and 2 outputs (infant mortality and life expectancy).
**FDH analysis, 2 inputs (hours per year in school, teachers per 100 students) and 1 output (PISA 2000 survey indicator).
Source: Afonso and St Aubyn (2004)

services such as day care. For each of these one can use a specific measure of performance. Yet combining all these performance indicators is not easy, as they do not measure the same thing. As an aggregate measure, we suggest seeing how the resources allocated to the welfare state achieve two of its main objectives, namely, alleviation of poverty and reduction of economic uncertainty.

We first proceed by looking at the cross-country relation between social spending and either poverty or income disparity. Poverty is measured by the percentage of households with adjusted[8] income below half the median adjusted income; income inequality is measured by the Gini index. Figures 8.2 and 8.3 provide the regression line for the two relations at hand. It is quite obvious that social spending exerts a clear-cut effect on both poverty and inequality.

---

[8] Adjusted for family size with appropriate equivalence scale.

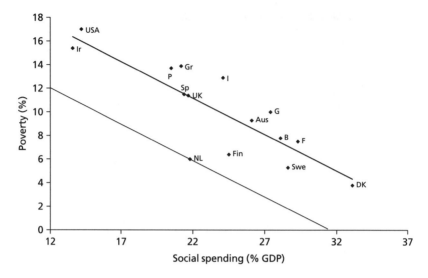

Figure 8.2. Social spending and poverty, 1994–2000

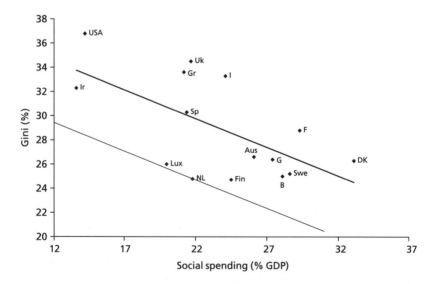

Figure 8.3. Social spending and income inequality, 1994–2000

The estimates are those given in Table 2.4. A test on the time stability of the estimated coefficients suggests that the impact of social spending on both dependent variables has not changed over time.[9]

---

[9] This is discussed in Gouyette and Pestieau (1999).

We should be cautious in interpreting these relations for a number of reasons. It is clear that reducing social inequalities and fighting poverty are not the only goals of social spending. At the same time, traditional measures of poverty and inequality based on the income of the households do not correctly reflect some of the outputs of social protection: health quality, feeling of security. Even more important, it is possible that countries with low poverty rates and low inequality have a strong preference for social protection, or that even before social protection intervenes, they have a rather equal distribution of wages.[10] In spite of these qualifications, it is tempting to use the statistical relationship already observed between social spending on the one hand, and poverty or inequality on the other, in order to construct an efficiency frontier and measure the efficiency of various welfare states. One could add that even if the causal relation were inverted, that is to say the degree of inequality explains the generosity of the welfare state, talking of inefficiency would still make sense.

To better grasp our approach, consider two countries that are identical in all respects but for the way their welfare state operates. In the first country, social spending is allocated towards the truly poor households, or towards those facing unexpected income losses; transfer programs, as well as the production of social services are run efficiently in terms of costs and resource utilization. In the second country, the picture is totally different: the Matthew effect prevails; administrative costs are rather high and productive efficiency in social services is low. It is quite clear that in aggregate terms, efficiency is greater in the first than in the second country and our aggregate measure reflects this difference. The assumption that these two countries are identical in all other respects is crucial.

Given that the relation between poverty or inequality and relative social spending is negative, the frontier has a negative slope. It is constructed by displacing the regression line downward so as to envelop all the data. The relative distance between this frontier and each country's performance can be viewed as a measure of its performance. If we take the example of the UK in Figure 8.2, with about the same amount of social spending this country could have attained a poverty rate of the Netherlands, 6 per cent instead of its actual 11.4 per cent.

The same reasoning could apply to the redistribution of income. In Figure 8.3, Spain and the Netherlands spend more or less the same fraction of their GDP on social protection, and yet in the Netherlands the Gini coefficient is lower than in Spain (0.25 vs. 0.30).

---

[10] For a critical evaluation of this approach, see Ravaillon (2001).

8.8 Conclusion

Among the critiques levelled against the welfare state, there is the inefficiency in distributing benefits and in producing services. This is often followed by a call for rolling back some programs and entrusting others to the private sector, the implicit assumption being that one can do as well with a leaner welfare state, and that the private sector is naturally more efficient. In this chapter we have tried to tackle the question of definition and measurement of the efficiency of the welfare state.

The welfare state consists of two types of programs: transfer programs such as welfare, social security, unemployment insurance, and the production of services such as hospitals, day care and schools. The issue of efficiency in transfer programs has to do with whether the transfers are made to the right people and whether the financial intermediation is cost efficient. The issue of efficiency in the provision of services can be expressed in terms of resource utilization. In other words, can we produce the same quantity and quality of services with less resources, or conversely, can we produce more and better services with the same amount of resources?

We have seen that there exist clear inefficiencies in the distribution of services. Because of administrative complexity or fear of stigmatization, the most needy people can fall outside of the protection of the welfare state. As far as the administrative cost of social insurance, particularly health and retirement insurance, a single public provider tends to be cheaper than a multiplicity of private firms. Finally, in the production of services, there are clear efficiency slacks, but they are not really dependent on ownership—public or private. What seems to matter is competition and autonomy.

The conclusion one can draw from this survey is clear. First, one has to fight the Matthew effect, and if this is not possible, one needs to make transfers transparent and universalistic. Secondly, one has to keep administrative costs at their current level, while at the same time maintain the quality of services provided. Thirdly, one has to introduce competition and autonomy in the management of social services. With an energetic efficiency-enhancing approach, the welfare state can recoup its credibility and recover desperately needed resources.

Within the expression 'welfare state', one tends to focus on 'welfare' and forget 'state.' An efficient functioning of the welfare state requires that the state, represented by the central government, play an important rule. Decentralization of decisions can be desirable for productive efficiency reasons. However, the main objectives of reduction of poverty and inequality across the national territory are to be entrusted to a central authority.

9 **Social versus private insurance**

KEY CONCEPTS

Adverse selection   new social question
commitment   self insurance
moral hazard

9.1 **Introduction**

Up to now we have been mainly concerned with social insurance, neglecting the role of private insurance as an alternative means of protection. In this chapter, we look at the role of the public versus the private sector in the provision of insurance in light of recent economic and social developments. We believe that the comparison between those two types of insurance cannot be addressed in the same way as 50 years ago, when the welfare state started. Social insurance is now experiencing a number of difficulties. Some of these are linked to recent developments such as fiscal competition, the declining credibility of the state, evolving labor markets, public opinion resisting redistributive policy, and an increasing demand for protection. First, let us clarify some conceptual issues, and give some figures for the evolution and the relative strength of social versus private insurance.[1]

9.2 **Social insurance**

9.2.1 THE STATE, THE MARKET AND THE FAMILY

The title of this chapter implies that the state and the market are the two institutions concerned with reducing the risks individuals face. In other words, we are neglecting the oldest and still important protection that is provided by

---

[1] See on this Poterba (1996) and Pestieau (1994).

the family.[2] Historically, the responsibility for providing security has rested with the family, or rather with the extended family or the 'village.' Risks such as disability, unemployment, retirement, or disease that are today essentially borne by social insurance programs, and those such as fire, street accidents and sudden death that are now borne by private insurance companies, used to be accommodated, at least partially, by the family or by the employer. Then came the private insurance industry to bring more adequate protection. Later, it was felt that the market was not providing appropriate coverage against some important risks; as a result governments became increasingly, indeed predominantly, involved in the provision of insurance.

Does that mean that the role of the family is now nil? Not really. Indeed, the family still plays an important insurance role that is widely documented in the study of altruism, exchange and bargaining within the family. In some instances, either it replaces the state or the market, or it offsets their action; in other instances, it has a rather supplementary role (Becker 1991, Kotlikoff and Spivak 1981). It is important to note that in countries that witness a retrenchment in social protection programs, there is an acute need for families to protect their members against risks such as loss of earnings. Some governments even tend to use family altruism as an alibi for cutting social protection spending.

9.2.2 THE SPECIFICITY OF SOCIAL INSURANCE

What is specific in social insurance relative to private insurance? As observed by Tony Atkinson (1996), there is no easy answer to this question. Is it the publicness of the provision? Not really—since one can have social insurance benefits distributed to individuals by private organizations. This is the case in Belgium for health care. On the other hand, in many countries such as France, there are a number of state-owned insurance companies involved in private insurance. Is the specificity of social insurance the mode of financing? Even though social insurance is often associated with the functioning of the labor market and financed by payroll taxes, there are countries such as Denmark where it is exclusively financed by general revenue. We should add, in this respect, that the decline in regular salaried employment contributes to loosening the link between social insurance and the labor market.

The most specific feature of social insurance is undoubtedly that it is mandatory and universal. But again, as stated by Stiglitz (1983b), one often confuses 'the question of whether individuals are to be insured with the question of who is to provide the insurance. The view that society must take measures

---

[2] This can be viewed as an extended from of self-insurance.

to ensure that everyone is insured against certain major risks does not, in itself, imply that the government should directly provide that insurance.' Yet, compulsion is not enough to characterize social insurance. In a number of countries car insurance and fire insurance are compulsory, and yet one does not consider this to be social insurance. This leads us to an additional specificity: social insurance is not based exclusively on an actuarially sound basis, but involves some redistribution. In other words, social insurance can be explained not only by a 'merit good' kind of argument but also by equity considerations. This latter feature is a prerequisite for universal access.

Two remarks are in order. First, even private insurance schemes are quite often forced to effect some redistribution. For example, life insurance companies are not always allowed to distinguish insurees according to sex or occupation. Hence, they redistribute from men to women, and from low life-expectancy occupations to high life-expectancy occupations. Secondly, the most extreme social insurance program, as far as redistribution is concerned, would be the proposal for a basic income scheme: a basic allowance would replace most social insurance transfers. As pointed out by Atkinson (1991), one should not speak of social insurance in that case. One could, however, speak of social protection without any attempt to mimic private insurance.

9.2.3 EXPENDITURE FOR INSURANCE, PRIVATE AND PUBLIC

In Figure 9.1 and Table 9.1, we contrast spending on social and on private insurance. This calls for three remarks. First, social insurance proxied by social protection dominates private insurance over time and across countries; it is almost five times as important. Secondly, in terms of trends, whereas social insurance seems to have reached a ceiling and even to have decreased in some countries, the role of private insurance is increasing everywhere steadily, even though slowly.[3]

Finally, looking at the cross-section presented in Figure 9.1, one notes two main features: a slight substitution effect with some countries relying more on private than on public insurance (Portugal, Spain and clearly Ireland) and others relying more on public than on private insurance (the Nordic countries) and two outliers for private insurance, the UK and Luxembourg.

---

[3] We are not trying to explain why private and above all social insurance developed at the end of the nineteenth century and particularly after 1945. According to Ewald (1986), the emergence of the welfare state is linked to the construction of social risks and to the reconfiguration of personal responsibility.

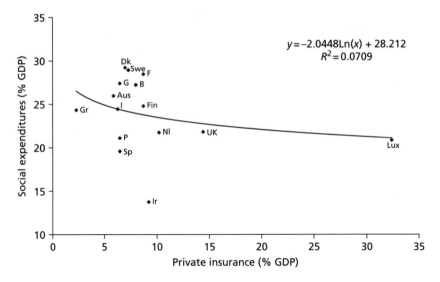

Figure 9.1. Social spending and private insurance as share of GDP, 2001
Source: Eurostat (2003)

Table 9.1. Social protection and private insurance in Europe, 2001 (% GDP)

Country	Private insurance	Social protection
Austria	5.9	26.0
Belgium	8.0	27.2
Denmark	7.0	29.2
Finland	8.7	24.8
France	8.7	28.5
Germany	6.5	27.2
Greece	2.3	24.3
Ireland	9.2	13.8
Italy	6.3	24.4
Luxembourg	32.4	20.8
Netherlands	10.2	21.8
Portugal	6.5	21.1
Spain	6.5	19.6
Sweden	7.3	28.9
United Kingdom	14.4	21.8

Source: Eurostat (2003)

9.3 Standard cases for social insurance

9.3.1 MARKET FAILURES

In general economists are interested by the failure of the market to provide adequate mechanisms allowing individuals to divest themselves of the risks they face, and by the role of the state in taking over some risk bearing. Quite interestingly, they are much more interested by this rather recent evolution than by the earlier one wherein the market progressively replaced the family in providing insurance protection. The standard examples of market failure are social risks, moral hazard and adverse selection.

Social risks are those risks faced by society as a whole and which are not diversifiable. Two types of social risks come to mind. First, there are all those low probability environmental or man-made hazards such as earthquakes, floods and large scale fires. Secondly, there are events such as wars or heavy recessions. As regards the first type of risks, individuals tend to have no interest in protecting themselves with insurance. They rely on society to help them in the unlikely case of a disaster, which in turn tends to affect their location decisions particularly in hazard-prone areas (Kunreuther 1978). We have here a typical case of moral hazard. Regarding the second type of risks, one often considers that society does better than an insurance firm, particularly by engaging in risk sharing across generations. Long term variations in public debt are often interpreted as a way of sharing the costs of wars or of heavy recessions between generations. It remains that most existing social insurance programs are not based on this argument of intergenerational risk taking. As to the first type of social risk, reinsurance could be the solution.

The *moral hazard* problem arises when the individual's incentives to avoid the insured-for event decrease as more insurance is provided. One consequence of this incentive problem is that insurance companies are reluctant to write unlimited insurance. It explains in part the limitations of insurance provided by the private market and the resulting reliance on social insurance. Note, however, that the government faces the same trade-offs between risk reduction and incentives as the market. On this ground the traditional family has a clear edge (Arnott and Stiglitz 1991) to the extent that members feel concerned as much by the welfare of the family as a whole as by their own welfare.

The problem of *adverse selection*, which confronts private insurance markets and leads to reliance on social risk-taking, arises because the insuree knows more about the likelihood of occurrence of the insured-for event than the insurer. There is thus an incentive for the worst risks to sign up for insurance and for the best risks to self-insure. The state has an advantage over the market because it can make insurance compulsory. In so doing, the problem of adverse selection is avoided but the insurance scheme is no longer actuarially fair: good risks pay for bad risks. It remains that making participation mandatory would suffice to solve the problem of adverse selections in private insurance markets.

The *administration* of privately-managed health or retirement insurance is often considered costly as we have seen in the previous chapter. As discussed in Chapter 8, this argument pertains to increasing returns to scale in transactions, and it is often used in favor of social insurance. Nobody will deny that these problems, social risks, moral hazard, adverse selection, and to a lesser extent increasing returns are serious imperfections of private insurance markets. The debate is whether or not public provision is an improvement. Some economists would argue that there are cases where social insurance is inferior to even poorly functioning private insurance arrangements. These are cases where 'non-market failures' arising from public provision of insurance are more severe than the private market failures it is alleged to address. Leonard and Zeckhauser (1983) argue, for example, that 'moral hazard may be a more significant problem for publicly provided insurance because there is less financial incentive for the government to structure its insurance contracts efficiently' (p. 150).

To sum up, the problem of moral hazard, adverse selection and social risks do not really make a convincing case for social insurance. As to the increasing returns argument, it mainly applies to health and old age insurance.

9.3.2 SOCIAL INSURANCE AS A REDISTRIBUTIVE DEVICE

There is a second type of rationale for social insurance that is also often questioned, namely the objective of redistribution. In an ideal world, what economists call a first-best redistribution ought to be achieved through non-distortionary income taxation that would include transfers to the needy. Indeed, such redistributive taxation has been presented as a sort of insurance contracted by individuals behind the veil of ignorance, that is, before knowing anything about, for example, their own ability, health status and other characteristics (Varian 1980). Then why use social insurance programs to achieve such redistributive goals and not rely on income taxation? The answer is that we do not live in a first-best, but rather in a second-best world where the government pursues its redistributive tax policy with little information about the individuals' characteristics. In such a world one can show that providing private goods including insurance benefits to everyone regardless of their contributions, can be desirable. This argument has been particularly developed for education, pensions and health insurance (Rochet 1991, Cremer and Gavahri 1997, Boadway and Marchand 1995, Cremer and Pestieau 1996, Boadway et al. 2003).

When talking about redistribution and social assistance, it is worth noting that some programs have targeted neither the poor nor the vulnerable, but rather the so-called 'losers.' Powerful groups in some countries, developing and developed ones, have demanded and received unemployment benefits and severance compensations as the price for agreeing to economic reforms. Those people are not usually the most needy in society. Yet their political voice is louder than that of the truly poor, and governments have often not been able to resist using such programs in order to gain political support (Fields and Mitchell 1993).

The argument of redistribution as social insurance can be fostered by an argument of altruistic externality. This latter argument is particularly used to justify the norm of universal access to health care. It applies less to the other types of social protection programs. When social insurance is mainly conceived as an instrument of redistribution, insuring people against poverty rather than against specific events such as unemployment or disability, the typical insuree is no longer a 'worker' but a 'citizen.' This raises the issue of entitlement. In a world of increased integration and cheap mobility, there is a natural trend to develop rules of exclusion. Witness the creation of a 'fortress Europe' that imposes barriers on East Europeans and Africans seeking entry to EU member states and access to employment and social protection (Brown and Crompton 1994).

9.4 **New arguments pro and con**

9.4.1 INCREASING DEMAND AND EVOLVING LABOR MARKET

To begin with, let us mention two rather recent developments that affect the balance between private and public insurance; they pertain to an increasing demand for social protection and to the changing condition of the labor market. In spite of political and financial pressure to limit the social insurance budget, there are factors that tend to contribute to more and more public intervention in the field of social protection. Population ageing and structural unemployment are clearly two problems of today's economies that call for increasing rather than decreasing the scope of social insurance.

At the same time, changing conditions in the labor market may affect the functioning of social insurance. As forcefully shown by Atkinson (1991), social insurance at least as far as unemployment and retirement are concerned is historically linked to the labor market. Its development has to be found not so much in the failure of private insurance markets, as in the need to improve the working of the industrial labor market. Good theoretical arguments can be presented to show that such an approach is well-founded. One clear implication of such a view of social insurance is that it is financed by payroll taxes paid by either employees or employers, or both. This raises a serious problem. The share of individuals benefitting from regular steady employment is declining and getting quite small in a large number of countries. Put another way, there are more and more inactive people, unemployed and self-employed workers and those with temporary jobs, and fewer and fewer salaried workers with steady employment.

In Europe, employment as a percentage of the working age is around 60 per cent. In Belgium this ratio was 53 per cent in 1989. Out of this

53 per cent, there were 10 per cent non-salaried workers and 7 per cent salaried workers with temporary or part-time jobs (Grubb and Webb 1993). This means that only 36 per cent of the working age population holds a steady salaried employment—too little to maintain a social insurance system based on labor market relations.

9.4.2 PAYROLL TAXATION, FISCAL COMPETITION AND SOCIAL DUMPING

In the traditional view of social insurance, most revenue comes from payroll taxes, that is a wage-based levy that increases labor cost. In a closed economy setting this does not raise any difficulty. However in an open economy, particularly in a world of increased economic integration and competition, there is pressure on firms to lower their production costs and will plead for limiting or even decreasing the social insurance budget. This phenomenon leads to what has been labeled 'social dumping', and results from fiscal competition. It occurs even when there is low labor mobility across countries. In a world without cooperation, each country competes for lower production costs and aims at ever decreasing payroll tax rates (See Chapter 6).

Two remarks on this: first, in countries where there is no direct link between the benefit and the revenue side, and where social insurance is financed by general (income and consumption) taxation, pressures for limiting social insurance are real, if not direct. Secondly, in countries where the link between the benefit side and the revenue side is tight, one could wonder why the agent cannot see through the social insurance mechanism that higher taxes imply higher benefits. After all, when an individual pays his car insurance premium he does not see it as a levy, but as a fair price for a particular service. This difference in perception between a payroll tax and an insurance premium is an important factor in the choice between one or another form of insurance.

There is another effect of globalization that affects the private insurance market. In an open economy it is increasingly difficult for government to impose regulations on private insurers that can be redistributive. For example, the legal impossibility to discriminate against individuals according to their risk class in private health insurance is likely to be desirable from a social welfare viewpoint. Such a regulation will not be implementable when 'healthy' people realize that they can do better by buying a cheaper insurance policy in a neighboring country. When this happens the government has to use other and less efficient redistributive tools.

9.4.3 CREDIBILITY AND COMMITMENT

Governments and parents both have the problem of commitment; they must bind themselves to courses of action they know to be desirable. For their own good, parents want to induce their children to be responsible, hence they restrict their protection to unavoidable risks. Yet, those children that Gary Becker (1991) calls 'rotten kids' have little incentive to abide by the rules as they know that their parents will be tempted to forgive them. Governments, particularly when they are responsive to citizens' concerns, are under constant pressure to move away from policies that are optimal in the long run. Two illustrations of this difficulty of commitment are public pensions schemes in some European countries, and the federal insurance of savings and loan institutions in the US.

The crisis in the US savings and loan industry is symptomatic of problems with many government insurance and guarantee programs. These problems involve moral hazard, if not fraud, and arise in both government and private sectors. However, they tend to be less severe in the latter because private corporations cannot sustain huge losses without going bankrupt, nor can they rely on the taxpayers to pay for their financial ineptitude. The money-making objective of private companies is quite different from the objectives of a government agency. A private company would have no trouble deciding to terminate a program that involves substantial losses even if the program's purpose is to protect the life savings of small depositors. Long-term contracts among private agents are an important source of efficiency of markets. State sovereignty makes such contracts unenforceable among successive governments.

In a related area, private life insurance companies will always handle retirement on a purely actuarial basis even if this implies providing meager benefits. A social security agency will have a terrible time resisting popular pressure if at some point the optimal pension scheme it adopted generates benefits that are deemed too low. Note that health insurance raises similar problems. With ageing and technology, the demand for health care is really skyrocketing. Even though some sort of rationing *à la Oregon* cannot be avoided, it is difficult for public programs to do it the only decent way: out in the open. As seen below, in that respect health care is a particular case in social insurance.

9.5 **Implications and conclusion**

Let us summarize the main points made in this chapter. Table 9.2 sketches the case for government versus market intervention in the field of insurance. First, one must realize that the public sector is subject to many of

Table 9.2. Comparative advantage of social over private insurance

Argument	Advantage
Large risk	nil when reinsurance is possible
Intergenerational smoothing	high
Moral hazard	negative
Adverse selection	nil if insurance is made mandatory
Administrative cost	noticeable particularly in the field of health care
Redistribution	high
Financing	negative because of tax competition and social dumping
Commitment	negative
Single provision	high in the field of health care

Source: Pestieau (1994)

the same incentive problems that lead to private insurance market failures. Secondly, on the revenue side, fiscal competition and economic integration make it increasingly more difficult to maintain 'generous' social protection programs regardless of their objective: insurance or assistance. Thirdly, the recent evolution of employment conditions leads to a widening gap between social protection programs and labor markets. Fourthly, recent economic and demographic developments call for increased public intervention in the area of redistributive income maintenance.

The lesson one can draw from these facts is clear. It is not sure that social insurance, or rather social protection, can pursue its two traditional objectives: insurance and assistance. Such a duality of objectives has not raised any difficulty in the past. Today, in a number of countries, it is unaffordable to provide insurance and at the same time take care of the needy. Furthermore, these objectives may interact inefficiently. On the one hand, redistribution is often used as a veil behind which allocative and even distributional dysfunctionings occur. On the other hand, sticking too closely to the insurance principle or, to put it differently, to the Bismarckian idea of social insurance, makes true redistribution impossible.

It has been shown that keeping the Bismarckian principle unchanged for the basic pension systems in France, Germany or Belgium, in a setting of demographic ageing and of pay-as-you-go financing, could rapidly lead to pockets of poverty among the elderly (Delhausse *et al.* 1993). For this reason, one should think of reshaping social protection in the direction of uniform transfers to all current beneficiaries of its various components. If these transfers were fixed at a decent level, the cost for public finance would be high, possibly higher than the current one. Individuals with middle or high income could supplement these transfers by private insurance programs (presumably without tax advantages).

Health insurance would also have this feature of universal access to a basic policy collectively decided. Diamond (1992) and others suggest combining universal access and competition among insurers and providers. The entire population would be divided into many large groups. Within each group, optimal social insurance principles could be applied with private insurance companies competing for these groups. Financing would be done by a combination of taxes and out-of-pocket payments for premiums and there would be some redistribution across groups. Within a group, selected insurance companies would offer supplementary policies to provide additional coverage for those who could afford it. In such a setting there would be no connection between health insurance and employment.

We believe that social protection should progressively abandon some of its insurance missions and focus on uniformity of benefits.[4] Financing should come from general revenue and be totally disconnected from the labor market. This way, private insurance would be allowed to provide additional coverage for those who found the basic policy insufficient and could afford to supplement it. Such a proposal is quite consistent with the three-pillars approach that is here extended to all traditional areas of social protection.

9.6 **Conclusion**

In this chapter we have shown that social protection is today facing a number of challenges that did not exist when it started fifty years ago: an ageing population, changing family structures, evolving labor markets, increasing individualism. Given these changes, it is by no means certain that social protection can attain its two traditional objectives of insurance and assistance. We argue that, while some insurance missions can be achieved by the market, assistance and redistribution can only be implemented by the state.

---

[4] This view is at odds with Barr (1992, 1998) who focuses on the insurance dimension of the welfare state.

10 Old age pensions

10.1 Introduction

In ageing Europe, pension systems are the social protection program receiving the widest attention. It appears that the cost of social protection programs depends not only on increasing longevity, but also on the effective age of retirement that, as we have seen in the last decades, has been decreasing in most European countries. Most pension systems in Europe are redistributive and based on pay-as-you-go financing. Therefore, we show that reforms are called for, but that they face huge political resistance. We also discuss the issue of privatization of pension systems, its reasons, and its limits.

10.2 Profile of the systems

Expenditures on pensions between 1980 and 1998 (in % of GDP) increased in all 15 European countries, except Ireland and Luxembourg. The largest increases in expenditure occurred in Greece and Italy. Today Austria, Belgium, Germany, Greece, France, Italy and Sweden all have relatively high shares of pension expenditure in GDP, while the UK and Ireland have relatively low shares compared to the EU15 average. Over the same period, all countries experienced some increase in the population aged 65 years and over, with the exception of Austria. Population ageing is likely to have a significant impact on pension expenditure over the next 20 years and beyond.

The link between demographic and social security benefits appears clearly in Figure 10.1. This figure is based on Table 10.1 which presents the relative

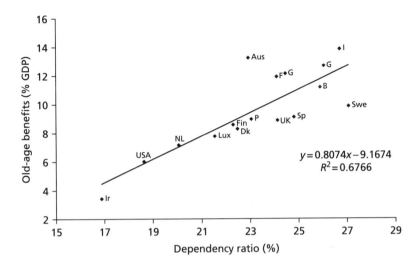

Figure 10.1. Old-age benefits and dependency ratio, 2000
Sources: OECD (2004a) and UN (2001)

share of old age benefits in 1980 and 2001 and the dependency ratio in 2001. The coefficient of correlation between old age benefits and dependency ratio is equal to 56 per cent. All European countries have some scheme to ensure that the elderly receive a certain level of income upon retirement—even in the absence of a sufficient contributions record. Those individuals with an appropriate contributions record are entitled to a social security pension. Social security, which is the word used in the US for public pensions, belongs to the first pillar of the pension system. There are generally three pillars.

The relative importance of the three pillars differ greatly across countries: the first being the statutory social security pension system, and the second and third pillars being contributions to supplementary collective and individual-ized pension funds, respectively. Expenditure on supplementary pensions has risen in all European countries since 1980. According to OECD (2000a) over the period 1990–96 their annual growth rate was 9.6 per cent. Of this expenditure on supplementary pensions, the level of voluntary contributions has risen to a greater extent than compulsory contributions. A comparison among European countries, however, is hampered by the fact that a pension scheme in one coun-try may contain elements of one or more pillars. Second-pillar supplementary schemes may be operated by the public sector and be compulsory, thereby containing elements of first-pillar pensions, or be operated completely within the private sector.

As we have seen earlier, one can distinguish two broad types of social secur-ity systems within the EU. The Beveridgean system, as practised in the UK, Ireland, Denmark and the Netherlands, ensures that all individuals are entitled

Table 10.1. Expenditure on old age pensions, 1980 and 2001

Country		Old age benefits (% of GDP)	Population aged 65+ (% of total)
Austria	1980	11.7	15.4
	2001	13.4	15.4
Belgium	1980	9.2	14.4
	2001	11.3	16.9
Denmark	1980	8.2	14.4
	2001	8.3	14.8
Finland	1980	6.1	12.0
	2001	8.9	15.0
France	1980	9.6	13.9
	2001	12.1	16.1
Germany	1980	10.9	15.5
	2001	12.1	16.6
Greece	1980	6.0	13.1
	2001	13.6	17.3
Ireland	1980	5.7	10.7
	2001	3.5	11.2
Italy	1980	9.7	12.9
	2001	13.9	18.2
Luxembourg	1980	10.6	13.6
	2001	8.1	13.9
Netherlands	1980	8.8	11.5
	2001	7.0	13.6
Portugal	1980	4.1	11.4
	2001	9.4	16.4
Spain	1980	6.4	14.0
	2001	8.9	16.9
Sweden	1980	8.4	16.3
	2001	9.8	17.2
United Kingdom	1980	7.3	14.9
	2001	8.7	15.6
United States	1980	6.2	11.3
	2001	6.1	12.7

Sources: Eurostat (2005) and OECD (2004a)
Note: Data on population for US 2001 is from 1998 instead

to a basic level of income upon retirement at a flat rate and independent of occupation. Private supplementary second-pillar pensions are most important in these countries, since individuals wish to ensure a certain replacement income upon retirement. The second system is the Bismarckian system from Germany, Belgium, France and southern European countries. In this system, contributions through employment generate entitlement to benefits. Benefits are closely linked to occupation and income. This division of systems has become less clear cut in recent years, however, and there has been a convergence between the two.

The financing of retirement benefits is generally through one of two means: 'pay-as-you-go' (PAYG), or funding. PAYG financing means that the current generation pays tax contributions to finance current payments to retired individuals. These contributions eventually add up to entitlement to pension benefits on retirement, but the link between contributions and benefits is rather loose. Fully funded pension schemes are characterized by employee contributions invested in a pension fund, which accordingly generates entitlement to a related benefit on retirement. First pillar pensions are generally financed on a PAYG basis, while both second and third pillars are funded (except in France for occupational pensions). In some countries there has been a shift away from PAYG-financed pension schemes towards fully funded schemes, in both the first and second pillars, as a response to pressures of an ageing population, and the growing liabilities of basic social security schemes.

10.3 **Financing problem**

The average income level of elderly people in most European countries is considered to be quite comfortable by historical standards, and by comparison with other age groups. This state of affairs is in great part due to public expenditure for old age pensions. Indeed, these constitute the main source of income of elderly households. As we have just seen, social security spending represents about 9 per cent of GDP, which is rather low for such an outcome. Yet, this situation is by no means sustainable, particularly in countries relying exclusively on PAYG. With PAYG one can express average pension benefit, p, as:

$$p = \frac{\tau w}{d},$$

where τ is the payroll tax, w, the wage level and d, the effective dependency rate (number of retirees divided by the number of workers). The effective dependency rate differs from the old-age dependency rate (number of persons aged over 65 to the working age population), as it takes into account both the unemployment rate and the effective retirement age.

To meet the above constraint when the old age dependency ratio increases (it is expected to double from 21.4 in 1990 to 42.8 in 2040 as a consequence of declining fertility and increasing longevity), some of the other variables must adjust:

- the contribution rate, τ
- the level of pension, p

- labor participation of the young and of the old
- the wage rate, that is, the productivity.

One can naturally count on other sources of income: capital income arising from pension funds or regular saving. One can consider the possibility of borrowing further at the expense of future generations. The problem of ageing in most EU countries is compounded by four problems: (i) diminishing the high replacement ratio (p/w) is politically hazardous; (ii) increasing the payroll tax is limited by tax competition; (iii) in the medium term at least, one expects a slowing down of productivity increase and/or an increase in the rate of non-employment; (iv) because of the Maastricht Treaty and also because most EU countries are already heavily indebted, more borrowing is unfeasible.

For six EU countries Table 10.2 presents some of the key features of their social security systems and their prospects. When comparing current pension benefits as share of GDP and the dependency ratio now and in 2030, one realizes that maintaining the current replacement ratio will be hard if nothing changes. The concept of activity rate between ages 55 and 65 reflects the fact that in these countries people tend to retire well before 65, the normal age of retirement (except in France). One can interpret this in two ways. The pessimist will say that these high figures reflect habits that will be difficult to change; the optimist will look at this evidence as showing available labor reserves that can be used as needed.

The next column gives the private pension funds assets as a percentage of GDP. This figure reflects the extent of collective precaution towards the future. It has to be contrasted with the following column, which yields the net present value of social security benefits minus contributions as a percentage of GDP (OECD 2000a). This net present value represents the hypothetical reserves that a funded system should have accumulated in order to generate the benefits to

Table 10.2. Features of social security in 6 EU countries

Country	Benefits (% GDP)	Old age dependency ratio			Employment (%) 55 to 65	Private pension funds assets (% GDP)	Net pension wealth (% GDP)
	2001	1980	2000	2050	2002	2000	1997
Belgium	11.3	21.9	25.9	51.2	26	6.0	115
France	12.1	21.9	24.5	46.7	34	–	40
Germany	12.1	23.7	24.1	54.7	38	3.0	45
Italy	13.9	20.4	26.7	68.1	29	4.0	105
Netherlands	7.0	17.4	20.1	45.0	42	113	55
UK	8.7	23.5	24.1	47.3	53	85	45

Sources: OECD (2000a, 2001b, 2004a), UN (2001), EC (2003)

which current and future retirees are entitled in the current social security system. It represents a liability identical to a public debt, and it reflects the amount of resources one would have to find if social security were to shift from a PAYG to a fully funded system.

We will study this issue in section 10.6. But first, let us come back to one characteristic of most EU countries, that is, the low participation rate of elderly workers.

10.4 **Early retirement**

The European welfare state aims at covering the basic needs of the old retirees with the basic social security program. This effectively restricts the labor force participation of the elderly up to age 65. Indeed, participation rates of those between 55 and 65 have declined steadily in a number of countries. This can be explained by the existence of benefit programs designed to cover loss of earnings due to unemployment and disability. Though not explicitly designed for this purpose, these benefit programs are used as exit routes from the labor force. Besides disability and unemployment, there are also two other exit routes. First, the social security scheme itself provides the possibility of withdrawing from the labor market before the mandatory age, with lower benefits in general. Secondly, mandatory early retirement schemes are introduced in cases of excess labor due to sectorial slumps, sometimes with the requirement that the vacancy be filled with a younger (and cheaper) unemployed person.

Clearly, early retirement and pension schemes in Europe are heterogeneous by nature. In some countries, such as the Netherlands, the exit route seems to be the disability program. In Belgium and in France early retirement programs are widely used. Many of these schemes were set up at the beginning of the eighties, at the time unemployment was rising throughout Europe, with the original intention of tightening the labor market. It would seem that this approach does not work. Countries with low actual retirement age have kept their high unemployment rates, even though some argue that, without this massive withdrawal from the labor market, unemployment would have been worse. In recent years, eligibility conditions into various programs have been restricted. This results in a shift to other programs, but rarely to a return to the labor market. What is clear is that elderly workers are sensitive to differential benefit entitlements, and choose their exit routes accordingly.

In a recent comparative study of the incentives to retire in 11 countries, Gruber and Wise (1999) show that there is a strong relationship between social security penalties on work and retirement.[1] The relationship is formalized in

---

[1] See also Blondal and Scarpetta (1998).

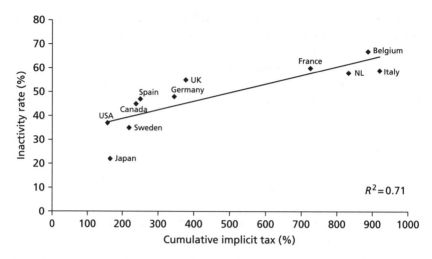

Figure 10.2. Implicit taxation and inactivity rate
Source: Gruber and Wise (1999)

Figure 10.2 which presents scatter plots of the sum of tax rates on continued work and the unused labor capacity between ages 55 and 65. The relation is clear. The solid line in the figures shows the fit of the data by a simple linear regression with a square term.

Why then are there such differences between these countries? Why does the government, in some countries, adopt these programs to encourage people to take early retirement? It certainly cannot be because countries have different preferences—some choosing shorter working lives than others. Nor can it be because of the drudgery of work, since there is no reason to think that work is harder in France or Germany than in the United States or Sweden. Instead, the explanation for these differences lies in features of the labor market itself. It is well known that the life-cycle fluctuations in wages do not correspond to fluctuations in productivity. At the start of a person's working life productivity will tend to exceed wages, whereas at the end the opposite is the case. This difference between wage and productivity seems to be wider in some countries than in others. One can show that in Belgium and France wages follow a clear rising trend through the life cycle, whereas in Sweden the curve is flat, and in Japan it is bell-shaped.

It can be clearly seen that in the former two countries employers have to encourage early retirement programs in order to rid themselves of expensive labor—costly, above all, in relation to its productivity. Furthermore, in some countries, there is a widespread belief in political and trade union circles that any early retirement of older workers creates vacancies for younger workers. This belief rests on the hypothesis of perfect substitutability between jobs for older and younger workers. But this hypothesis is debatable. It is now widely recognized that sending older workers into retirement in order to stimulate employment among the young does not work and may even be counter-productive. In fact, certain recent empirical studies show that this type of policy has usually failed (Boldrin *et al.* 1999, Snessens *et al.* 2003). These two observations tell us that if the trend towards early retirement is to be reversed, a revolution is needed in the mentality of the countries concerned. Economic agents, employers' organizations, trade unions and governments must be persuaded to adopt wage scales that more closely match productivity. They must also give up the belief that there is a direct link between early retirement and jobs for the young unemployed.

Yet, it would be naive to think that a drastic reduction of implicit taxes on postponed activity would suffice to increase the activity rate of elderly workers. Such a reduction should have to be accompanied by active employment policies in a number of areas: training of ageing workers, legal barriers to age discrimination, employment subsidies and, as already mentioned, a better match between wage and productivity. On these matters the successful experience of countries such as Sweden, and more recently Finland, could be used as guidelines for countries plagued by too early retirement.

10.5 **Difficult reforms**

It would be tempting to applaud current trends. After all, the lowering of the age of retirement and the long-term reduction of the working week are signs of progress. But this continually growing period of inactivity has to be funded. All the projections show that without urgent reform the ageing of the population will bring about a worrisome impasse.

Another way of illustrating the cost of older people's low rate of labor market participation is to calculate what, theoretically, would have been gained if they had continued to work up to the age of 65. Herbertson and Orszag (2003) have performed this calculation for several countries, and found that these theoretical gains represent more than 10 per cent of GDP in Germany, France and Belgium, as illustrated in Table 10.3. Despite the need to reform the retirement system, most countries exhibit resistance to any kind of change and a strong preference for the *status quo*. There are a lot of surveys that show not only that workers are fond of their retirement system, but also that they are opposed to the slightest reform, especially if it could lead to raising the standard retirement age (Fenge and Pestieau 2005).

Earlier we characterized as ill-founded the belief that early retirement fosters youth employment. Yet beliefs can be stronger than facts in shaping economic policies. The 2002 Eurobarometer addresses precisely this question. Answers are given in Figure 10.3 which shows that in 9 out of 15 EU countries more

Table 10.3. Cost of early retirement (% GDP)

	1990	2000	2010
Austria	–	14.4	15.9
Belgium	15.2	14.1	17.9
Denmark	6.9	8.2	11.3
Finland	9.6	10.6	15.8
France	11.2	10.3	15.2
Germany	9.5	13.2	12.6
Greece	10.4	10.7	11.2
Ireland	6.9	6.8	8.9
Luxembourg	12.5	12.6	15.1
Netherlands	10.5	11.2	15.7
Portugal	9.1	8.6	9.4
Spain	9.7	9.3	11.1
Sweden	4.7	5.2	7.5
United Kingdom	7.5	7.2	10.1
USA	5.4	5.7	8.1

Source: Herbertson and Orszag (2003)

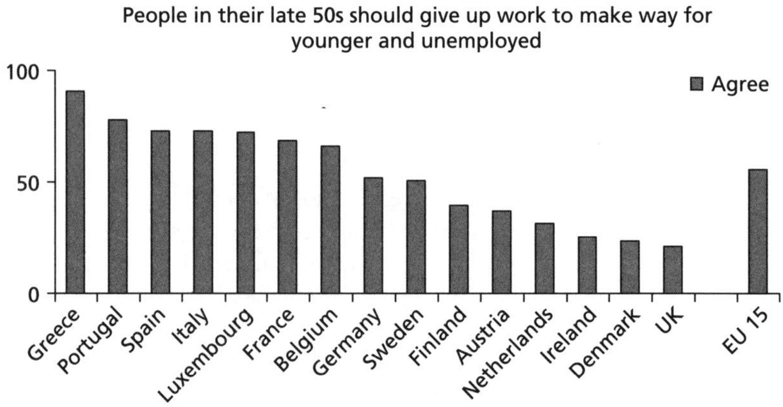

Figure 10.3. Perceived intergenerational redistribution
Source: EC (2003)

than half the population believes that elderly workers help the young and the unemployed workers by exiting the labor force. Countries where this perception is particularly strong belong to the southern part of Europe where early retirement is pervasive and reforms are strongly opposed.

The pension problem is quite often considered as being mainly demographic. In fact, it is as political as demographic.[2] During the last four decades there has been an increase in the dependency ratio, namely in the relative number of people aged 65. At the same time, the effective retirement age has

---

[2] See on this Cremer and Pestieau (2000).

Table 10.4. Age of effective retirement and life expectancy

	Men				Women			
	Life expectancy		Retirement age		Life expectancy		Retirement age	
	1960–65	95–2000	1960	2000	1960–65	95–2000	1960	2000
Belgium	67.9	73.8	63.3	57.6	73.9	80.6	60.8	57.4
France	67.6	74.2	64.5	58.5	74.5	82.0	65.8	59.5
Germany	67.4	73.9	65.2	60.7	72.9	80.2	62.3	59.7
Ireland	68.4	73.6	68.1	63.4	72.3	79.2	70.8	65.6
Italy	67.4	75.0	64.5	59.3	72.6	81.2	62.0	58.3
Spain	67.9	74.5	67.9	60.9	72.7	81.5	68.0	61.2
Sweden	71.6	76.3	66.0	62.1	75.6	80.8	63.4	61.4
UK	67.9	74.5	66.2	60.5	73.8	79.8	62.7	60.4

Sources: UN (1998), Burniaux *et al.* (2004), Blondal and Scarpetta (1998)

been declining and this is not a demographic phenomenon. In France, for example, over a period of some 40 years, the length of retirement has grown from an average of 3.2 years to 15 years for men, and from 8.6 years to 23.7 for women as shown in Table 10.4. But this growth, and the length and therefore the cost of retirement, are due as much to the decline in the rate of activity of older workers as to their increased longevity.

10.6 **Reforming social security**

The heavy reliance on the pay-as-you-go pensions provision has been justified during the decades of rapid growth in population and productivity. However, with the prospect of an unprecedented ageing of the population, combined with a decline in productivity growth, one has the feeling that shifting to fully funded schemes would contribute to avoiding unbearable pressure on public finance. Indeed, such a shift is known to have a huge short-run cost because the transition generation is thus forced to pay twice: for its own retirement through the fully funded scheme, and for the generation to be retired through the pay-as-you-go scheme. What we should have done to avoid this double burden was to keep and to invest the contributions paid by the working generation when the pay-as-you-go method was first introduced, instead of transferring it to the retired generation that had not contributed to it. In other words, we shouldn't have given a 'free lunch' to that generation (Belan and Pestieau 1999). But precisely the purpose of this 'free lunch' was to provide resources to a generation of retirees that had gone through the great depression and the Second World War.

To illustrate the difficulties facing most social security systems, the example of the US is quite useful. Past and current retirees have recovered much more from social security than they and their employers contributed even allowing for a reasonable rate of return. A man with average earnings who retired in 1980 could expect to receive benefits 3.7 times what his contributions would have generated, had they been invested in low-risk government bonds. The ratio was even higher for women (4.4), and much higher for lower income people. There was some redistribution within cohorts of retirees, but that intragenerational redistribution was dominated by the intergenerational redistribution. As the system reached maturity and the dependency rate (ratio of beneficiaries to workers) continued to increase, the ratio of social security benefits to taxes paid declined.

Now a large number of households, primarily of higher earners, judge their mandatory social security contributions to be a poor investment. In other words, as the windfall gain caused by the immaturity of the system vanishes, together with a growth rate superior to the financial rate of return, the pay-as-you-go and the redistributive features of social security cease to be attractive to an increasing number of households. Hence, the political base begins to splinter along incomes lines.

This story illustrates well the vulnerability of mandatory social security in terms of its two key features: it is redistributive and unfunded. If a reform is just restricted to moving from unfunded to fully funded financing, little can be done. Hence most proposals include a progressive abandonment of intragenerational redistribution. In so doing the political backing of a reform is to be obtained along age and income lines. Given that social security reform is unlikely to be Pareto improving, it is important to understand who the winners and who the losers are. The purpose of this section is to clarify this issue. Indeed a social security system can be characterized by a number of features as presented in Table 10.5.

1. Fully funded or pay-as-you-go financing principles, the latter allowing for some intergenerational redistribution. In the large majority of countries the main public scheme is unfunded, and supplementary schemes are private and fully funded (France is a rare exception).

2. Sources of financing retirement: wage related contributions paid by employees and employers or government funds (general taxation).

3. With the pay-as-you-go method, there is intergenerational redistribution, which tends to benefit older generations and not necessarily the needier ones.

4. Social security can cover the whole population with a minimum pension for people without entitlements; it can also be restricted to a minority of individuals holding steady employment.

5. Social security can effect some intragenerational redistribution, for example, by giving a uniform pension to everyone. In case of actuarial fairness there is no such redistribution.

Table 10.5. Characteristics of social security systems (polar cases)

Characteristics	Polar cases	
financing principle	pay-as-you-go	funding
financing sources	contributions wage related	general taxation
intergenerational redistribution	strong	nil
universality	universal coverage	restricted coverage
intragenerational redistribution	flat benefits*	actuarial fairness
organization	public (involving unions & management)	private
accounts	collective	individualized
efficiency	strong distortions	few distortions
what is defined	defined benefits	defined contributions
annuitization	mandatory	optional
trust	nil	strong

* with sometimes means tests

6. Besides the traditional dichotomy between public and private organiz-ation, there is the possibility of employer/employee joint responsibility (e.g. collective agreements and industry-wide bipartisan approach).

7. Accounts can be individualized in such a way that for each worker there is perfect transparency in the linkage between contribution and expected benefits.

8. The allocative distortions of social security depend on the above fea-tures; they are likely to be minimized with a contribution-linked benefits formula, individualized accounts and fully-funded financing. Then social security contributions are viewed just like any other private insurance premium.

9. We can distinguish among systems where contributions are fixed or where benefits are fixed, or at least defined with respect to current wages.

10. There are systems with mandatory annuitization and others with optional annuitization. Public pensions always imply annuitization; this is one of their comparative advantages.

11. Finally, there is the crucial issue of trust in the system. Do people expect to receive what they feel entitled to?

To sum up, it is quite clear that there is a close interdependence between those characteristics. For example, as already alluded to, distortions are likely to be negligible in a system with actuarial fairness; defined benefits are easier with pay-as-you-go and public organization. Intergenerational redistribu-tion is impossible with funding. Universal coverage is easier with a public organization. At the same time, one can have actuarial fairness with the pay-as-you-go method; a public system can be funded and have individualized accounts.

Table 10.6. Two typical social security regimes

	Bismarckian	Chilean
financing principle	pay-as-you-go	funding
financing sources	mostly contributions	wage related contributions
intergenerational redistribution	to the benefit of older generations	nil
universality	universal coverage	restricted coverage
intragenerational redistribution	earnings-linked benefits	actuarial fairness
organization	unions & management (with public control)	private
accounts	collective	individualized
efficiency	strong distortions	few distortions
what is defined	defined benefits	defined contributions*
annuitization	mandatory	optional
trust	low	high in the beginning

* guaranteed minimum pension

On the basis of this taxonomy Table 10.6 opposes two polar systems: an ideal system from the 'Continental' (Bismarckian) viewpoint widely accepted just after World War II, and an extreme form of privatized social security as in Chile. In most proposed reforms of social security systems, the key issue is that of shifting from the pay-as-you-go method to fully funding in order to allegedly foster saving and meet financial difficulties. In fact, along with that shift most reforms include a move towards less intragenerational redistribution, indi-vidualized accounts, privatization and defined contributions schemes. These latter aspects are, to a large extent, much more important and disruptive than a simple shift from unfunded to funded systems. Indeed, one can show that such a shift is rather innocuous under some assumptions.

Finally it is important to insist on a rather obvious point which is that in terms of social security reforms, the US and even more so Chile, offer a political and economic setting quite different from that of France or Italy.

What can we conclude from this discussion? It is clear that reforms are needed. So it is likely that progressively European governments will move towards a flat rate benefit system publicly financed by PAYG, as well as a private fully funded and actuarially fair scheme. What is important is to understand that such a reform will be socially costly, but surely less so than the status quo or than a drastic and hasty privatization.

10.7 **Conclusion**

Most EU countries are today experiencing high standards of living among their elderly. This is due mainly to quite generous social security benefits. Except in the UK and the Netherlands, the contribution of supplementary private pensions to what is called the 'golden age of the elderly' is negligible. Another characteristic of the EU is the low effective retirement age. This, combined with increased longevity and low productivity increase, makes the future of social security rather gloomy. Obvious reforms are needed, as regards postponing retirement and reducing benefits. But these reforms face hard opposition from various vested interests. It is easy to find a majority of elderly and close-to-retirement voters who oppose any reform. Yet if nothing changes, poverty among the elderly could come back in a number of countries such as France, Italy and Germany[3] (Pestieau 2003a,b).

Finally, it is important to note that moving from pay-as-you-go to fully funded schemes, or from public to private systems, will only be a solution if the benefit rules are modified. In that case some problems can be solved, but at the cost of some victims—most likely low income families. It is essential to understand that the pay-as-you-go method is in part responsible for the current crisis only because when it was started, contributions were offered to the then retirees. This debt then incurred has to be refunded now.

[3]   See the World Bank's manifesto on a Chilean type of social security, in World Bank (1999).

11 Health care

11.1 Introduction

Dealing with health care is quite different from dealing with unemployment, disability or retirement. Health care is a unique commodity for a number of reasons. First of all, receiving it can be a matter of life or death and is thus subject to less economic rationality than other consumptions: health has no price. Also, health care spending has increased in recent decades more rapidly than most other social spending. Yet, what makes health care so different is undoubtedly the issue of incomplete information that generates moral hazard and adverse selection problems. It is also the paternalistic argument according to which people should be forced to have medical insurance for their own good, even against their own will. These specificities make it difficult to tackle the issue of cost containment and to face the urgent need for reform that most European countries now face. In the following, we first describe the recent evolution of health care spending. We then turn to the issue of cost containment and of reform.

11.2 Expenditure on health care

Health spending reported in Figure 3.3 seems to be relatively steady over the period 1978–98. This is not the case for what appears in Table 11.1 and Figure 11.2 for two reasons. First the health spending figures we are using in this chapter do not include sick leave, maternity leave, work accidents, disability which is the case of health spending. These items seem to have a dampening effect. Secondly, spending on health and health care in most European countries has risen dramatically over the period 1997–2002. Combined with lower

Table 11.1. Total spending on health and the relative part of public spending, 2001–02

Country	Total spending on health (% GDP)			Public health spending (% total)		
	2001	2002	change 82–02	2001	2002	change 82–02
Austria	7.6	7.7	16.6	68.5	69.9	−7.2
Belgium	9.0	9.1	28.1	71.4	71.2	n.a.
Denmark	8.6	8.8	−5.3	82.6	83.1	−5.0
Finland	7.0	7.3	8.9	75.5	75.7	−5.3
France	9.4	9.7	n.a.	75.9	76.0	n.a.
Germany	10.8	10.9	22.4	78.6	78.5	0.3
Greece	9.4	9.5	n.a.	53.1	52.9	n.a.
Ireland	6.9	7.3	−6.4	75.6	75.2	−6.5
Italy	8.3	8.5	n.a.	76.0	75.6	n.a.
Luxembourg	5.9	6.2	3.3	89.8	85.4	−8.1
Netherlands	8.5	9.1	15.1	n.a.	n.a.	n.a.
Portugal	9.3	9.3	57.6	70.6	70.5	25.4
Spain	7.5	7.6	33.3	71.3	71.4	−10.0
Sweden	8.8	9.2	−1.0	84.9	85.3	−6.8
UK	7.5	7.7	32.7	83.0	83.4	−4.7
US	13.9	14.6	48.9	44.9	44.9	10.0

Source: OECD (2004c)

economic growth the increase in health spending has driven the share of health expenditure as a percentage of GDP up from an average 7.8 in 1997 to 8.5 in 2002. This is in sharp contrast to the period 1992–97 when the share of GDP spent on health remained almost unchanged.

Over the short period 1997–2003 the US far outstripped EU15 with health expenditure growing 2.3 times faster than GDP and rising from 13 per cent to 14.6 per cent.

For the longer time period 1982–2002, health expenditure as percentage of GDP changed very differently across EU15 from 57.6 in Portugal to −6.4 in Ireland. Figure 11.1 gives the evolution of health care spending in the EU15 over the period 1980–2002. From 1980 to 1989 the share of health care spending in GDP has slightly decreased. There was a quick increase between 1992 and 1997 and a new dramatic rise. These evolutions are not the same across countries. Figures 11.1(a) and (b) also show the evolution of spending in some EU15 countries. One sees that the increase is quite sensible in the larger countries such as Spain, France and Germany. Denmark, Sweden and Ireland, all smaller countries, were the only ones to experience a decline in health care spending as a percentage of GDP. The growth in health expenditure was in part, a deliberate policy in a country such as the UK, which realized that cost containment during the mid-1990s had strained its health care systems.

The rapid growth of expenditure in France was largely the result of structural factors in the health care system. *Ex post* reimbursement of health care expenditure by sickness insurance funds created little incentive to control health care expenditure and to raise efficiency within the system.

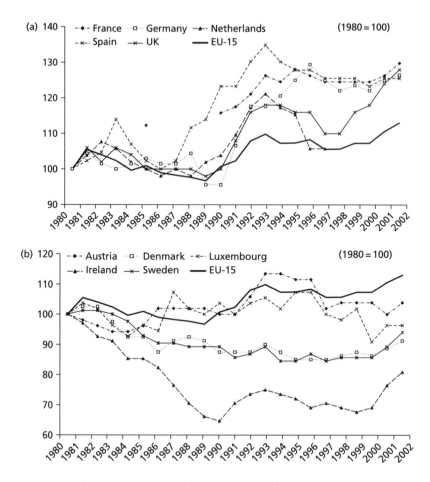

Figure 11.1. Public health spending. (a) High spending (b) Low spending
Source: OECD (2004c)

The future development of health care systems in Europe is likely to be influenced by the continued drive for efficiency and cost containment. Growth in private sector medicine is an important feature in the recent development of health care systems. As Table 11.2 indicates, the public share of health expenditure has decreased in most countries over the period 1982–2002. It increased in Portugal quite a lot (25%) and slightly in Germany. To explain the rapid expansion of medical spending a number of factors are often cited: ageing of population, income growth, third party payment, administrative costs, rapid advances in medical technologies and rising public expectations.

As already seen, the share of population aged 65 and older is increasing everywhere in the EU. As the population ages, one expects health care expenditure to

Table 11.2. Public expenditure on health: coverage and cost sharing, 1981–90

Country	% of covered population		% of cost sharing	
	1990	change 81–90 (%)	1990	change 81–90 (%)
Austria	99	0	84	0
Belgium	98	−1.0	87	−1.1
Denmark	100	0	85	0
Finland	100	0	82	−2.5
France	99.5	0.5	75.1	0.1
Germany	92.2	2.4	92	−3.2
Greece	100	13.6	85	0
Ireland	100	0	90	−3.2
Italy	100	0	75.9	−4.4
Luxembourg	100	0	91	0
Netherlands	69	−7.6	71.3	−7.0
Portugal	100	0	n.a.	n.a.
Spain	99	17.9	90	0
Sweden	100	0	94	−1.6
United Kingdom	100	0	93	0
United States	44	4.8	61	0

Source: Besley and Gouveia (1994)

increase as well. To the extent that the demand for medical care increases with income and faster than income increases, one thinks that the increase in health expenditure is in part a manifestation of a richer society wanting more health care. One also expects that the third party payment, which implies that only a negligible fraction of medical costs is paid by patients out of their pocket, can explain a fraction of the growth in medical expenditure. Administrative costs have also increased relatively faster than GDP.

There is now a wide consensus that these factors, ageing, income growth, third-party payment and administrative costs can, at best, explain 40 per cent of the increase in medical expenditure. Accordingly, most of this increase is due to technological improvements: physician training, medical techniques, and equipment all of which have improved over time and will continue to do so in the future. This technology-based theory helps explain the increase observed in countries with different health care systems. All these countries have one thing in common—they all have been exposed to the same expensive innovation in technology. Clearly, it is important to understand the main sources of growth in expenditure in the debate on cost containment and on health care reforms.

Health care systems in the EU share common features:

- third-party payment;
- single provider approach that implies offering all citizens, regardless of contribution and health status, a determined set of health services at low cost, if any;

- cost-based reimbursement: in most cases, health care providers are paid on the basis of the actual costs of treatment as opposed to capitation reimbursement. This latter technique used in the UK and in health maintenance organizations (HMO) gives each health care provider an annual payment for each patient in his or her care.

Health care systems in European countries differ in their source of financing, coverage and means of delivering benefits. The Nordic countries, the UK, and Ireland finance health care systems largely from general taxation. Other countries have predominantly insurance-based systems or a mixture of the two. Countries with insurance-based systems: Belgium, France, the Netherlands, Germany and Luxembourg, tend to have higher shares of expenditure on health care systems. This may be a result of higher quality care, or, more likely, a lower degree of control over expenditure and cost containment that is characteristic of an insurance-based system.

Access to some level of health care services in European countries is universal for all individuals. Individuals may opt out of obligations to state health care systems in Portugal or Italy by taking out supplementary coverage. In other European countries supplementary insurance is available, but contributions to the state health care system remain obligatory. Countries with a large degree of insurance financing in health care systems tend to have a larger market of private health care providers. In tax-financed schemes the private market tends to be relatively less well developed.

One of the difficulties in assessing the performance of health care systems is how to measure their output. Just using indicators such as life-expectancy or mortality is clearly insufficient; it misses the qualitative dimension that is so important. One has to consider not only the number of years added to one's life but also their quality. Health economists are thus using the concept of quality-adjusted life years (QUALYS). It is, nevertheless, interesting to check whether there is any relation between health and health care spending. There is no clear relation between output indicators such as life expectancy at birth, healthy life expectancy, potential life years lost due to premature mortality or infant mortality, and total costs of health care and input indicators such as total expenditure on health or total health employment. As seen above, one reason might be inefficiency.[1] Another reason may be that quality aspects are neglected for lack of data. In any case it is well known that the nature of the environment and of the food diet is likely to affect those demographic indicators more than most health care spending, as is forcefully argued by Illich (1997) who mentioned the case of Greece spending hardly 5 per cent of GDP for health care for a life expectancy that is well above that of the USA, which at that time spent almost 3 times more.

[1] See Osterkamp (2004).

11.3 **Cost containment**

Even though European countries spend much less than the US, both in rel-ative and in absolute terms, cost containment is a priority. Since the early 1980s, governments have tried a number of strategies to reduce health care costs. Among the measures taken or discussed, are the move from cost-based reimbursement to capitation, the introduction of managed competition, the explicit introduction of quotas and the increased participation of well-to-do patients.

The movement towards capitation formulas and more generally to health maintenance organization is under way in a number of countries. It is clear that cost-based reimbursement does not induce economizing on methods for delivering health care. But, at the same time, capitation-based reimbursement creates incentives to provide lower quality services. Managed competition is a combination of government regulation and market economy. The essen-tial idea is to band people into large organizations that require health care providers, and even insurance companies to compete on price and quality to obtain their business. Co-insurance is increasingly imposed for two reasons. One is to curb moral hazard problems that lead to incremental costs. The other is to bring additional resources into the system. In a number of countries, coin-surance is quasi nil for low-income households and some categories such as the retired or the disabled. It can even increase with the income or wealth of households as it does in Belgium.

When constraints are imposed on the supply side of the system, which is unavoidable in a single-provider country, rationing, whether implicit or expli-cit, is necessary. For equity and efficiency reasons it should be made explicit. In that respect the Oregon experience is of great interest. Among the cost containment policies the most delicate is, undoubtedly, the one pertaining to quotas. Every day tough choices are made, but generally they are implicitly based on *ad hoc* rules such as first come first served, or geographical distance. In 1990 the state of Oregon in the USA, decided to tackle head-on the problem of expensive care for the many, and of little health care for some. The state decided to rank about 1600 medical procedures with a computer program that would balance the costs and benefits of these procedures. The objective was to eliminate coverage for those treatments that were disproportionately expensive. So doing, the state could double the number of poor people who were eligible for Medicaid, the government program of basic health insurance for the poor.

Of course the list of covered treatments was controversial. Implementing it inevitably meant that the state would have to refuse to help some people who so far benefited from certain medical treatments, and that some of those people would die sooner than they otherwise would. Oregon tax payers were not ready to provide everyone with all the medical care they could ever want. Scarcity cannot be avoided. In not implementing the Oregon list (which was the case), other choices were made that were socially less desirable but politically more acceptable, since they were made in the secrecy of the medical office. The Oregon plan proposed to shift spending medical care spending to treatments that provided greater public health benefits. Its failure illustrates the difficulty of rational reform and the constant need to search for political feasibility.

11.4 **Equity aspects**

As Table 11.3 shows, public health care covers the entirety of the population in most European countries. The only exceptions are the Netherlands and Germany where well-to-do households, the income of which is higher than a specified amount, are covered by well regulated private health insurance. In other words everyone is covered for a wide range of health care. This does not mean that health consumption is fairly allocated. Health is a good which is not evenly distributed across individuals of a given group and furthermore it varies across income groups. In a kernel, one can easily obtain a negative correlation

Table 11.3. Public health care coverage

Country	% of covered population		
	1962	1982	2002*
Austria	78.0	99.0	97.0
Belgium	62.1	99.7	99.0
Denmark	95.0	100.0	100.0
Finland	55.0	100.0	100.0
France	n.a.	99.2	99.9
Germany	85.9	91.8	90.9
Greece	44.0	88.0	100.0
Ireland	85.0	100.0	100.0
Italy	88.0	100.0	100.0
Luxembourg	99.0	99.8	99.6
Netherlands	71.0	73.8	75.7
Portugal	20.0	100.0	100.0
Spain	54.0	85.5	99.8
Sweden	100.0	100.0	100.0
United Kingdom	100.0	100.0	100.0
United States	n.a.	n.a.	25.3

* Last year available is 1997 for Spain and Italy, 2000 for Ireland, and 2001 for the Netherlands and the United States.

Source: OECD (2004c)

between mortality rates and income. However, the relation between morbidity and income is less clear. Thanks to self-assessed scores, Van Doorslaer *et al.* (1997) obtain a strongly negative statistical relation between income and morbidity. Does that mean that one has the same negative relation between income and consumption of medical services? Not really. There is instead a positive but not significant relation between the two.

The financial side is slightly easier to handle.[2] The question raised here is that of the distributive incidence of health financing in the EU. If it can be shown that health financing is not regressive, namely that health spending, public and private, as a percentage of household income does not decrease with income, we can conclude that the welfare state fulfils its redistributive objective in this particular area. In such a study we have to consider the various sources of public finance but also expenditure from private insurance contributions and out-of-pocket payments. Not surprisingly countries that rely upon private sources tend to be regressive. Out-of-pocket payments are expectedly regressive everywhere and private insurance payments tend to be progressive only when they are supplementary to public financing. As to public financing itself, progressivity is expected particularly when it relies on income or payroll taxes and not on indirect taxes. Table 11.4 gives the (Kakwani) redistributive indices for a number of European countries plus the US. Negativity (positivity) implies regressivity (progressivity). As one may observe a lot of countries have near proportional financing systems. Countries relying on public financing and specifically on direct levies have a progressive system. This is the case of the UK, Italy and Finland.

Table 11.4. Redistributive indices for the financing source of health care

	Public finance	Private finance	Total
Belgium (1997)	0.061	−0.250	0.000
Denmark (1987)	0.037	−0.236	−0.005
Finland (1994)	0.066	−0.198	0.060
France (1989)	0.111	−0.305	0.001
Greece (1989)	−0.053	−0.007	−0.045
Ireland (1987)	–	−0.096	–
Italy (1991)	0.071	−0.061	0.041
Netherlands (1989)	0.060	0.015	−0.035
Portugal (1990)	0.072	−0.228	−0.045
Spain (1990)	0.051	−0.163	0.000
Sweden (1990)	0.010	−0.240	−0.016
UK (1993)	0.079	−0.095	0.051
US (1987)	0.106	−0.317	−0.130

Source: De Graeve and Van Ourti (2003)

[2] See De Graeve and Van Ourti (2003).

11.5 **Conclusion**

It is clear that health care is in need of serious reform. The nature of this reform will depend on what the objectives are: purely budgetary, or with a strong concern for equity. There is increasing pressure to move towards at least partial privatization. It is important to keep in mind the pros and the cons of such a move. Table 11.5 summarizes the comparative advantages of private over public intervention. The case for a predominant public pillar supplemented by private insurance remains very strong.

Table 11.5. Comparative advantages of private versus public health care insurance

Characteristics	Public insurance	Private insurance
Open to self selection	No	Yes (in general)
Redistribution across risk classes	Yes	No (in general)
Redistribution across income classes	Yes	No
Equitable access	Yes	No
Open to moral hazard	Yes	Yes
Nature of contract	Collective and political	Individual and short-term
Preference matching	Weak	Yes
Administrative cost	Low	High
Competitive challenge	No	Yes

12 Unemployment and poverty

12.1 Introduction

The labor market is at the heart of our welfare states for a number of reasons. First, it is the source of income for the majority of households. Secondly, most social insurance schemes were initially designed within the labor market arrangements. This is surely the case for not only unemployment insurance, but also retirement and disability insurance. In many countries, both benefits and contributions are settled through paritary negotiations involving both unions and management with the state playing an increasingly active role of third party. Finally, as we have already seen there is an interaction between the state of the labor market, the level of wages and employment, and the nature of social protection. One of the key issues in today's economies is how to keep a balance between the need for firms to adapt to ever-changing market conditions and workers' employment security. What is fascinating with an overlook of the EU labor market performance is to realize that the trade-off between income security and employment does not really exist. There are countries which have succeeded in achieving both.

12.2 Unemployment and employment

Surprisingly the rates of employment and unemployment do not reflect the same reality. The rate of unemployment is the ratio of employed workers over the labor force that is the sum of employed and unemployed workers. The employment rate (also called ratio) is the number of employed workers over the working age population (e.g. persons aged 25–64). In the denominator one thus finds the labor force but also all the people who are for whatever reason not involved in paid work: students, housewives, (early) retirees, disabled, and so on. For that reason, one minus the rate of employment is much higher than the rate of unemployment and better reflects the idea of unused capacity. Recent data for the EU15 and the US are given in Table 12.1. The participation rate (also called the labor force participation rate) is given. Denoting u, the unemployment ratio, e, the employment rate and a, the activity rate, these concepts are defined and related as follows:

$$u = \frac{\text{unemployed workers}}{\text{employed} + \text{unemployed workers}}$$

$$e = \frac{\text{employed workers}}{\text{working age population}}$$

$$a = \frac{\text{employed} + \text{unemployed workers}}{\text{working age population}}$$

and thus:

$$a = \frac{e}{1 - u}.$$

The unemployment rate is the better-known concept; it is precise, and quite well agreed upon. As already seen, it is an indicator of social exclusion and it most often implies the payment of unemployment compensations. As Table 12.1 shows, it is on average higher in the EU than in the US. There is a wide dispersion across countries with a low 3.6 per cent for the Netherlands and a high 11.4 per cent for Spain. The Scandinavian and Anglo-Saxon countries plus Luxembourg and Austria do quite well, better than the US, whereas the four large continental countries, Spain, France, Germany and Italy have disappointing records. As is shown later the hedge of the US over the EU is new. High unemployment is not a European trait; until the end of the 1960s unemployment was very low in Europe and the talk then was of the European unemployment miracle. The miracle came to an end in the 1970s when unemployment steadily increased. It kept increasing in the 1980s and in spite of a slight decline in the mid 1990s it is on average very high with large cross-country differences.

It is often believed that unemployment rates do not reflect the true state of non-employment as it does not comprise people who are more or less discreetly pushed out of the labor force: students beyond a certain age, soldiers, housewives, early retirees. Moreover, it does not take into account that the same rate of unemployment can hide different situations regarding temporary

Table 12.1. Employment, activity and unemployment rates. Persons aged 15–64 (%)—EU15 2003

	Employment rate	Activity rate	Unemployment rate
Austria	68.2	71.6	4.7
Belgium	59.3	64.3	7.7
Denmark	75.1	79.4	5.5
Finland	67.4	74.1	9.1
France	61.9	68.2	9.3
Germany	64.6	71.3	9.4
Greece	58.0	63.8	9.1
Ireland	65.0	68.0	4.5
Italy	56.2	61.6	8.7
Luxembourg*	63.6	65.3	2.6
Netherlands	73.6	76.4	3.6
Portugal	67.1	72.0	6.8
Spain	60.7	68.5	11.4
Sweden	74.3	78.9	5.8
United Kingdom	72.9	76.6	4.9
United States	71.2	75.8	6.1
EU15	64.8	70.3	7.8

* 2002

Source: OECD (2004d)

and part-time work. To meet the first questioning, one increasingly uses the employment ratio.

Here again, it is much lower in the EU (64.8%) than in the US (71.2%) with large cross-country differences. Belgium, Greece, and Italy have a ratio below 60 per cent; France and Spain are below 62 per cent. At the other extreme, Denmark, the Netherlands, Sweden and the UK outbest the US. We have already discussed one of the main factors of low employment ratios: the low rate of activity of aged workers. In 2003, the employment ratio for male workers aged 55 to 64 was 42.3 per cent in the EU15. It was 38.5 per cent in 1990 showing some improvement. In the US, it was 59.9 per cent in 2003.

The employment ratio does not say much about work intensity, namely the number of hours of work in a year. In 2003, France, followed by Italy, Belgium, the Netherlands and Germany, was leading in terms of the lowest number of hours per capita. The annual number of hours ranged from 611 hours per capita in France to 800 in Portugal, which is also the average for the OECD countries. This figure results from two main effects: the employment ratio effect just seen and the number of hours per worker. The case of the Netherlands is interesting: it has a high employment ratio and at the same time the lowest number of hours per worker in the EU which leads to quite a low number of hours per capita. As shown in the OECD (2004d), there is a negative cross-country correlation between the employment ratio and average annual hours per worker implying that each country reacts differently, intensively or extensively, to improvements in productivity and living standards.

12.3 **Unemployment benefits**

Protection against unemployment in all European countries predominantly takes the form of cash benefits. Contributions paid in work generate entitlement to unemployment insurance benefits. These benefits tend to be income-related in countries which adopt Bismarckian principles of social insurance. For unemployed individuals whose employment record does not entitle them to unemployment benefits, or who have exhausted their entitlement, a social assistance or minimum safety-net benefit is available in all European countries. This benefit is generally means-tested and unlimited in duration, although additional criteria may be attached. Unemployment benefit systems differ considerably across European countries in terms of entitlement criteria for benefits, ease of obtaining entitlement, duration of payment of benefit and the existence of requirements to work and participation in active labor market programs.

Table 12.2 shows unemployment benefits as a share of GDP for the EU15. All European countries experienced a rise over the period 1980–2000 with a lot of fluctuations corresponding to the employment cycles. As Figure 3.3 (p. 28) shows the peak was reached in 1993.

Unemployment compensations as well as early retirement programs for labor market reasons are passive benefits. They do not contribute to fostering employment as opposed to active spending aimed at training, subsidizing

Table 12.2. Public expenditure in labor market programs in the EU (% of GDP)

Country	Year	Total	Active measures	Unemployment compensation*
Austria	2002	1.78	0.53	1.12
Belgium	2002	3.65	1.25	1.94
Denmark	2000	4.63	1.28	1.37
Finland	2002	3.07	1.01	1.53
France	2002	3.06	1.25	1.63
Germany	2002	3.31	1.18	2.10
Greece	1998	0.93	0.46	0.47
Ireland	2001	1.83	0.70	0.83
Italy	2002	1.20	0.54	0.57
Netherlands	2002	3.56	1.85	1.72
Portugal	2000	1.51	0.61	0.69
Spain	2002	2.42	0.87	1.55
Sweden	2002	2.45	1.40	1.04
United Kingdom	2002–03	0.75	0.37	0.37
United States	2002–03	0.71	0.14	0.57

* Passive measure includes unemployment compensations and early retirement schemes developed for labor market reasons.
Source: OECD (2004d)

employment or financing public employment. In recent years, one observes a certain convergence between the continental European welfare states and the Anglo-Saxon liberal welfare states towards adopting direct wage subsidies for low-wage earners. These measures as well as those devoted to training have a positive effect on employment.[1]

The passive nature of labor market programs is also apparent in the reluctance of controlling the job-seeking behavior of the unemployed. In countries such as Belgium or France, there is a popular aversion to check whether beneficiaries of unemployment insurance are willing to work or to ascertain that they are not performing illicit work. At the end of the 1990s, the number of sanctions for insufficient willingness to work as a percentage of all unemployed beneficiaries was about 1 per cent in Belgium, 2 per cent in Denmark, 5.5 per cent in the UK, 7.3 per cent in Norway and 10.2 per cent in Finland (OECD 2000b).

To conclude this section, there is a certain agreement that passive spending might hurt employment and active spending foster it. Yet, econometric evidence is not as clear-cut as this widely agreed-on conjecture.

12.4 **Two tracks**

The unemployment benefit program is only one component of social protection 'at large' that pertains to employment.[2] One can also mention disability benefits schemes, early retirement provision and the safety-net welfare system. Furthermore, most European countries have a legal minimum wage policy and employment regulations.

Standard minimum wage policy requires employers to pay a minimum wage rate (or a minimum weekly wage for full-time workers) to employees irrespective of their education, skill, training or productivity. This policy typically applies to all workers, including school dropouts without work experience, and recipients of unemployment and disability benefits should they decide to return to work. Some countries achieve an effective minimum wage arrangement through more or less comprehensive collective bargaining agreements. In a few countries some groups of workers are not covered by minimum wage laws; in others (e.g. the Netherlands) wages below the minimum are permitted for some groups (e.g. young workers).

Employment regulations constrain the ability of employers to alter the size of their work force in response to changes in the demand for their output; hence, an employment contract becomes a fixed cost to the employer generating caution in the addition of permanent workers to the enterprise. Such

---

[1] See section 5.4.   [2] See Haveman (1997).

regulations also lead to disguised unemployment in periods or places of slack demand, as employers are constrained from firing workers, even if there is insufficient demand to keep them.

The constellation of policies yielding full coverage and a generous and accessible safety net of social protection has both positive and negative economic impact related to the comprehensiveness, generosity and accessibility of the system. For a long time only the positive impact was emphasized: reduction of poverty and income disparity; protection for severe income losses; quality of employer–employee relationships; efficient job search and employment match.

However, for the last decade the negative effects have become increasingly apparent: reduction in the labor demand for low wage, low-skilled individuals; substitution of temporary employees for permanent workers; reduction in the willingness to work and in the incentive to engage in job search; increase in the costs of enterprises; mounting rigidities in the labor market. These adverse effects of generous and accessible income protection policies are even more serious if the income protection policies are loosely structured, poorly integrated or ill managed. Numerous examples of such program inefficiencies have been documented in the literature. These include: the failure to detect voluntary job-quitting as a basis for benefit claims, or concealed employment among beneficiaries of unemployment programs, or benefit reduction (marginal tax) rates equal to or approaching 100 per cent in some assistance programs.

All together these policies, which characterize most European countries, have the following implications: high unemployment and joblessness, slow employment growth, low and steady wage inequality and relatively high wage growth. By contrast, the North America package consists of low minimum wage, modest social protection and few barriers to hiring, firing and geographical mobility leading to rapid employment growth. As an example, in the early nineties the minimum wage in the Netherlands and France stood at over 50 per cent of the average wage, while in the USA it was roughly 35 per cent of the average wage. As a result, as illustrated in Figures 12.1 and 12.2, one is left with a tough choice between North American wage stagnation and West European double-digit unemployment.

Figures 12.1 and 12.2 illustrate well the existence of two tracks regarding the evolution of employment, wage and inequality. The economies of the USA and the UK (to which one could add Ireland, Australia and New Zealand) have been creating a lot of jobs at the cost of wage stagnation and high poverty. Western Europe's economies feature growing wages and low poverty levels, but they have generated few new jobs.

Since 1960 North American employment has increased by nearly 60 per cent while jobs in the European Community have increased by less than 15 per cent. During the same period, the 10 per cent real wage growth of the USA contrasts with real wage growth of nearly 60 per cent in the European Community.

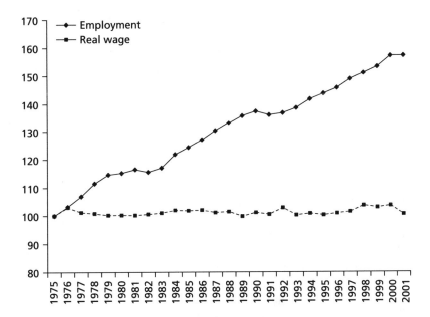

Figure 12.1. Employment and real wage USA 1975 =100

Source: OECD (2004e)

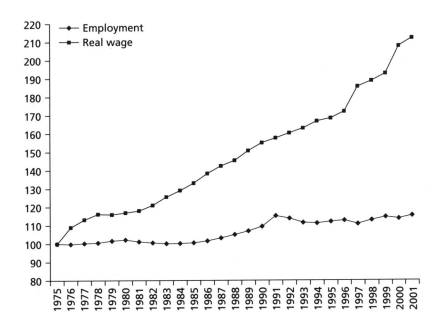

Figure 12.2. Employment and real wage EU15 1975 =100

Source: OECD (2004e)

The high and accessible level of income protection benefits and high min-imum wages in Europe have successfully maintained a relative low level of inequality. Figures for the late 1980s indicate the Gini coefficient for the USA at 34.1 and for the UK and Ireland at 31.7, while that for the six founding EU countries stood at 26.6 and that for the Scandinavian countries at 22 (Atkinson *et al.* 1995). The same holds for the poverty rates. They are lower in the EU than in the US. While evidence on changes is mixed for the EU, in the US the level of official income poverty has risen substantially.

Are we thus facing a tough alternative between wage stagnation and double digit unemployment? Or, as Haveman (1995) puts it, are there alternative approaches to social policy that could simultaneously address the two prob-lems? Haveman thus suggests a combination of measures that together assure both adequate income support to those without sufficient earnings and the attainment of full employment. Without looking further at Haveman's pro-posal and that of others, three remarks are in order. First, with people as they are, one cannot avoid the 'iron law' of income support, that is, the unavoidable trade-off between the level of minimum income guarantee and the severity of work disincentives. Secondly, as we learn from political scientists, the choice of the North American or Western European track, or the adoption of a third way, is entrenched in the political and economic culture of the countries concerned. Thirdly, the choice is not a real one. We believe that the Western European track is not sustainable. If nothing happens it would eventually imply both unemployment and poverty.

Over the last years employment protection legislation (EPL) has been scru-tinized by the OECD which developed a measure of its strictness. It seems that over the last decades a process of partial convergence has taken place as regard to EPL. This process was driven by an easing of regulation in the countries where EPL was relatively strict. Yet the relative position of countries across the overall spectrum of EPL strictness is stable: Portugal (3.5), Spain (3.1) and France (2.9) being the strictest and the UK (1.1) and Ireland (1.3) the loosest (see OECD (2004d)). The scores in parentheses are for 2003. The US has a score of 0.7. EPL is shown to protect existing jobs and to reduce the reemployment chance of unemployed workers. Thus the net impact of EPL on aggregate unemployment is theoretically ambiguous. Empirically, it can be shown that strict EPL hurts employment of youth and prime-age women. It also contributes to long term unemployment.

In a recent paper, Blanchard and Tirole (2004) study employment protec-tion in France where EPL is particularly strict and unemployment high. They observe an increasingly dual and unequal labor market with two classes of workers, those on permanent contracts and those on temporary ones. They look for a good reform that would let firms be free to lay off a worker but would make them pay a lay-off tax. How does this compare to the way employment protection is currently designed in France? In France, as in a number of other Continental European countries, unemployment contributions are collected through a payroll tax, not a lay-off tax. This means that firms that lay off more workers do not pay more. At the same time, the judicial system may prevent firms from laying off workers.

Blanchard and Tirole thus suggest a shift from a payroll tax to a lay-off tax, and in exchange, a reduction in the role of judges. How could it be done? The answer comes from the system of experience rating in the US, which is a bit ironical. The US are indeed the only country in the OECD where employers' social security contributions are partially 'experience rated', that is to say they are calculated partly on the basis of the lay-off activity of the firm: a firm's tax rate is determined by individual status based on the unemployment insurance benefits paid to workers it has recently laid off. The main motivation of experience rating is to prevent firms from using unemployment insurance as a subsidy to temporary lay-offs and to avoid dual labor markets.

Coming back to Europe, there are countries which over the last years have been successful in terms of low unemployment and low poverty. In that respect, Denmark's example is worth noting. In Denmark, one finds both low unemployment rates and low poverty rates thanks to what is called the Danish *flexicurity* approach (OECD 2004d). This approach combines flexibility (a high degree of job mobility thanks to low EPL), social security (a generous system of unemployment benefits) and active labor market (training and monitoring of the unemployed). This model thus points out to a third way between the Anglo-Saxon model with low EPL, low unemployment, but little social protection and the strict EPL characterizing Southern European countries with high unemployment rates and not necessarily low poverty rates.

The results of the Danish *flexicurity* approach are very attractive. Are countries such as Spain, France and Belgium ready to adopt the means to achieve them—basically an active social policy with generous but temporary unemployment benefits linked to mandatory training and search for employment? This is surely a timely question. Recent reforms in Belgium indicate that the answer might eventually be positive.

12.5 The working poor in Europe

On Continental Europe it is typical to think of the poor as non-working people such as the unemployed, pensioners and children—or at least as people whose ability to work is restricted, such as single parents. If this were so, wages and other employment legislation would ensure that the working poor were an exception whereas in the US they are fairly prevalent. In fact, as we now show, in the EU a substantial share of the poor work, and a majority of the poor live in households with at least one member working. The term 'working poor' is somewhat ambiguous. At the very least it means that the individual works

Table 12.3. Working poor in the EU. Poverty rates in 1996

Country	Poverty rates			Share among all poor	
	All	Employed households	Employed	Employed	Full time employed
Austria	9.9	9.2	6.3	27.8	20.1
Belgium	11.4	8.3	5.7	19.2	14.0
Denmark	7.3	5.4	4.7	31.2	14.6
Finland	11.7	8.6	7.2	22.9	17.5
France	16.8	14.7	9.2	21.7	15.0
Germany	9.1	7.7	5.5	27.4	15.5
Greece	22.1	18.8	16.2	26.3	21.4
Ireland	20.4	16.1	10.8	19.5	13.2
Italy	16.7	16.2	10.6	21.6	17.3
Luxembourg	13.3	13.4	8.6	25.8	21.7
Netherlands	12.3	11.9	7.9	28.0	16.9
Portugal	26.9	24.7	21.8	36.7	30.5
Spain	19.6	16.3	12.2	19.8	16.2
United Kingdom	24.5	14.3	9.4	17.0	9.9
EU14	16.4	13.3	9.0	22.2	15.5

Source: Strengmann-Kuhn (2002)

and belongs to a poor household. The ambiguity resides in whether or not we include all the household members and whether or not we are only concerned with full time workers.

Table 12.3 presents some data from the European Community Households Panel (ECHP) for the year 1996. We can distinguish three types of individuals: workers, members of households with at least one worker, and all other individuals. For all the EU15 countries except Sweden (EU14), the average rate of poverty is 16.4 per cent for all households, 13.3 per cent for the members of households with at least one employed and 9.0 per cent for the employed. The rate of poverty is based on half the average income and on the OECD equivalence scale.

These data differ from those presented in Chapter 2; they come from a different source and concern a different year. Yet the pattern is unchanged. Overall poverty is highest in Portugal, the UK, Ireland and Greece and lowest in Denmark, Austria and Germany. Poverty rates in households with employed people are also highest in Portugal, Ireland and Greece—but not in the UK, which is an interesting result. They are lowest in countries in which poverty rates are also low for the whole population. It is interesting to see the share of the working poor among all poor in the EU. Focusing on the working poor *per se*, and not the number of poor households with workers, we have in the EU15, 22 per cent of all poor who are working and 15 per cent who are working full time. That share is lowest in the UK where 17 per cent of the poor are employed and only 10 per cent of them are employed full time; the highest share of working poor is found in

Portugal—36.7 per cent and 30.5 per cent, respectively. If, instead of focusing on the workers themselves, we consider the households they belong to, the figures are much higher: 61 per cent for employed and 50 per cent for full time employed.

One clearly sees that the employment status (full time or not) is important. Yet, even full time workers can be poor. Does that mean that their wage is insufficient? In part, yes. But the main reason is that they do not live alone. A wage may be quite sufficient for a single individual, but much too low for 4-persons households, even with the appropriate equivalence scale. In other words there are two ways for a worker to be poor: low pay and family size.

Strengmann-Kuhn (2002) distinguishes those two sources of poverty. He shows that the majority of the working poor is poor because of the household size. For the whole of the 14 EU countries shown, 73 per cent of the working poor would not be poor if they were living alone. Low pay is a source of poverty among workers in Germany, the UK and Denmark. Family size is the main source of poverty among workers in Belgium (94%) and Portugal (90%). Even though the relation between the rate of unemployment and of that of poverty is not clearly determined, there is a clear positive relation between the rate of low-wage employment and poverty (Marx and Verbist 1997). In other words, poverty is arising from lack of jobs or from underpaid jobs.

In the UK and in the US (and soon it will apply in many other countries), there is a strong tendency to move from welfare to workfare. In a recent book, Solow (1998) studies the consequences of workfare policies—more precisely the effects of withdrawing welfare benefits and forcing the former recipients into the labor market. His analysis is based on common sense economic reasoning and on some experimental 'workfare' initiatives on the part of several American states. His main conclusion is that the sponsors of welfare reform are kidding themselves. A reasonable end to welfare as it prevails in the US will be much more costly in budgetary resources, and also in the strain on institutions, than any of the advocates of workfare have been willing to admit. As one can already observe in the US, the welfare rolls are diminishing. Yet one cannot avoid the question of what has happened to the former welfare recipients and to the working poor. They may be living with relatives who cannot afford to keep them, or on the street, or in shelters. After all, the goal of a welfare reform hopefully is not just to provide apparently comforting data. Yet, this is what happens in countries where the administrative system tracks only welfare recipients and not the would-have-beens.

Solow shows that a decent welfare-to-work transition requires a more complicated and more expensive set of changes than current reform proposals. These changes imply the creation of an adequate number of jobs for displaced welfare recipients—even in today's US with full employment, such jobs are lacking—as well as the recognition that many welfare recipients simply have to combine earnings and public assistance if they are to lead tolerable lives.

12.6 **Conclusion**

In this chapter we have seen that unemployment insurance is not the only social program that covers people out of work. Disability insurance, paid sick leaves, early retirement schemes represent more money and cover more people than unemployment compensation in some countries. Yet, the relation between the number of people out of work and the generosity of these alternative schemes has not been well established.

We have also noted the split between countries such as the UK and the US that have experienced a huge increase in employment along with a quasi-stable level of real wages over the past decades, and countries of the Continental European Union which have experienced the reverse pattern—stable employment and growing real wages.

Finally, even though the working poor are more frequent in countries with lean social protection, one notices that over the past years countries known for the generosity of their welfare state also count an increasing number of working poor. These are workers, mostly young people and women, who have temporary or precarious jobs.

In view of these three observations, we believe that the challenge facing European governments is to adopt policies that can induce those people who can work to work, while assisting those who cannot. We have here the infamous distinctions between the *deserving* and the *undeserving* poor, or between the *voluntary* and the *involuntary* unemployed. So we come back to the difficulty, if not the impossibility, of sorting out these two categories in a world of imperfect information and of self-interested behavior.

Among the policies suggested, there is the earning income tax credit (EITC) and work sharing. Comparing their relative merits is quite irrelevant as they apply to different views of unemployment. Work sharing starts from the idea that the pool of employment is fixed, at least in the short run, and that therefore there is no way to expand it. EITC does work where unemployment is voluntary, specifically when it is due to the existence of a poverty/unemployment trap.

In this chapter we have hardly discussed the role of unions. In most EU countries there has been a steady decline in trade union density. Only four countries increased their density since 1970: Belgium, Finland, Denmark and Sweden. These are countries where unemployment benefit as a rule is administered by union affiliated institutions. The role of unions density and the more or less centralized level of bargaining between unions and management have been widely discussed in the literature but without clear-cut conclusions regarding their effect on unemployment. The one robust relationship one obtains is that overall earnings dispersion tends to fall as union density, bargaining coverage and centralization/coordination increase. These are equity aspects that are worth being considered carefully.

13 Family allowances

KEY CONCEPTS

Childcare   parental leave
family allowance

13.1 Introduction

In this chapter, we study the effect of family allowances on poverty within the European Union. While there appears to be a remarkably redistributive effect, family allowances are only one component of child policies. Their objective is not just poverty alleviation, they also aim at fostering female employment and fertility. Sharp differences exist in the level and pattern of child policies across European countries, the Nordic countries leading the pack in terms of generosity.

13.2 Evolution and structure

Family allowances are available in all European countries, although their generosity and their benefit rule vary across countries. The share of expenditure on family allowances is far from being as important as that of the big two components of social spending, health and retirement. Yet, as this chapter shows, its incidence on income inequality and poverty is quite impressive. In that respect family allowances are likely to be one of the most efficient social programs in terms of Euros spent.

On average, between 1980 and 1998, the share of expenditure on family benefits actually fell in European countries from 2.1 per cent to 1.8 per cent of GDP. This fall is largely due to the declining number of children as a fraction of the total population. As a consequence, expenditure per person (in % of GDP per capita) has been at a steady 8.6 per cent. This figure is relatively high in countries such as Denmark, Germany or the UK, and low in the Southern European countries like Greece or Spain.

Table 13.1. Family allowances in 2001

	Family allowances (% of GDP)	
	Sensu largo	*Sensu stricto*
Austria	2.92	0.67
Belgium	2.31	1.70
Denmark	3.79	1.00
Finland	3.01	1.02
France	2.81	1.06
Germany	1.91	0.78
Greece	1.83	0.65
Ireland	1.63	0.63
Italy	0.98	0.47
Luxembourg	3.44	–
Netherlands	1.14	0.71
Portugal	1.15	0.41
Spain	0.50	0.13
Sweden	2.92	0.93
United Kingdom	2.23	0.09
United States	0.38	0.10

Source: OECD (2004a)

Even though the data used in international comparisons covers not only family allowances, but also other transfers such as maternity benefits, in this chapter, we focus on family allowances *sensu stricto*: that is the universal benefit paid to the parents (often the mother) or the guardian of dependent children. With this narrower definition, Belgium and Germany are the biggest spenders, and Spain the smallest as it appears in Table 13.1.

In most countries child allowances are universal; most often per child benefits increase with the number of children and with the age of the child. There are few cases of means-tested benefits. Even though today everyone agrees that the main function of family allowances is to help families with children—that is to avoid child poverty and to implement some horizontal redistribution between families with and without children—it was introduced in some countries as a way of encouraging fertility. France is typical of such a dual approach; family allowances only start after the second child.

What the ideal pattern of family allowances in relation to age, family size and income should be is not clear. Public finance is astonishingly silent on this matter. The main lesson to emerge from the existing scanty work is that family allowance cannot just be restricted to horizontal equity; they also affect vertical redistribution in a world where redistributive taxation is heavily constrained. Political science and political economy have emphasized the key role of universal family allowance in terms of political support to the welfare state. Indeed, flat rate family allowances represent one of the few programs which

Table 13.2. Tax privileges and family allowances in France and Germany

# children	Couples with one earner			Couples with two earners, the second earning 1/3 of average income		
	1	2	3	1	2	3
Germany						
Difference to a couple with one child less (in %)	8.2	6.9	6.5	6.3	5.9	5.9
France						
Difference to a couple with one child less (in %)	0.8	7.7	9.1	1.1	7.4	7.5

Source: Meister and Ochel (2003)

reaches a wide range of social groups. This holds in particular for the middle-aged and well-to-do healthy households that do not draw any benefits from unemployment, health care, social security or welfare programs. This positive and non-normative argument explains, in part, why the French government decided to drop the means-tested benefit rule adopted a year ago and revert to universalism.

Family allowances are also to be contrasted with the use of children's allowances as part of the direct tax system. Family allowances are more egalitarian than these tax advantages, as the poorest parents may lack sufficient income to benefit from them. At the same time, family allowances, being tax-exempted, are criticized as favoring the top income brackets subject to high marginal tax rates. One might mention a recent comparison between Germany and France, which takes into account both tax privileges and family allowances, and show how they differ between the two countries for different family size and different earnings structure. The reference income is the average income in both countries.

Child allowances represent the chunk of benefits. Given that in France they are only awarded for 2 children and more, we see in Table 13.2 that the largest marginal advantage is for having one child in Germany and three in France. Benefits are also relatively higher for couples with one earner than for couples with two earners. Table 13.3 presents the relative advantage of having two children instead of none in the EU. The difference is large ranging from 18.7 in Austria to 1.9 in Spain. The overall advantage also varies according to the number of children as the comparison between France and Germany shows. This raises a key question. If one believes that family benefits hardly affect fertility and have mainly a redistributive impact, why is there discrimination against one-child families?

Table 13.3. Tax privileges and benefits for married couples with two children* in 2000

	Additional net income with two children (%)
Austria	18.7
Belgium	15.4
Denmark	8.5
Finland	10.0
France	8.6
Germany	12.7
Greece	7.8
Ireland	4.2
Italy	4.9
Netherlands	6.9
Portugal	6.9
Spain	1.9
Sweden	9.7
United Kingdom	6.6
United States	6.8

* Two employees with gross incomes of 100% and 33.33% of an average production worker's wage.

Source: Meister and Ochel (2003)

13.3 **The two effects of family allowances**

We are interested by the incidence of family allowances on poverty. Our data basis is that of the LIS (Luxembourg Income Study) which gives us information on 10 members of the EU. The first question is that of the incidence of family allowances on the poverty rate for the whole population and for the children. Clearly, the incidence of family allowances depends on three factors: the generosity of the program, the benefit rule and the correlation between income and family size. Therefore we will look at the incidence of family allowances, assuming that each country devotes to them the same fraction of GDP or the same amount of Euros.

As in previous chapters, we choose to measure poverty by the percentage of households below half the median income. Income is the amount of resources reported in the panels used by the LIS. The equivalence scale is the standard OECD scale: 1 for the first adult; 0.7 for the others; 0.5 for each child.

Table 13.4 yields the actual poverty rates in 9 members of the EU and the hypothetical rates, assuming that there are no family allowances. The difference is an indicator of the efficiency of family allowances at reducing poverty. That efficiency score varies a lot, ranging from 3.7 in Ireland to 0.3 in Sweden. More specifically, we can distinguish a group of countries with high

Table 13.4. Family allowances and poverty

Country	Year	With allowances	Without allowances	Efficiency score
Belgium	1992	4.2	7.2	3.0
Denmark	1992	6.3	7.0	0.7
Finland	1991	7.0	7.9	0.9
France	1989	8.7	10.9	2.2
Germany	1994	7.7	8.5	0.9
Ireland	1987	8.1	11.8	3.7
Luxembourg	1994	4.1	6.3	2.2
Netherlands	1991	5.5	6.4	0.9
Sweden	1992	7.8	8.1	0.3
UK	1995	10.8	12.8	2.0

Source: LIS

Table 13.5. Family allowances and poverty among children

Country	Year	With allowances	Without allowances	Efficiency score
Belgium	1992	2.6	13.8	11.2
Denmark	1992	2.9	6.0	3.1
Finland	1991	1.6	5.2	3.6
France	1989	6.9	16.9	10.0
Germany	1994	8.0	12.0	4.0
Ireland	1987	9.3	19.1	9.8
Luxembourg	1994	2.8	11.8	9.0
Netherlands	1991	5.2	8.9	3.7
Sweden	1992	2.3	4.2	1.9
UK	1995	15.5	23.1	7.6

Source: LIS

efficiency: Ireland, Belgium, Luxembourg, France and the UK, and countries with low efficiency: Sweden, Denmark, Finland, Germany and the Netherlands.

Table 13.5 focuses on the poverty rate among children. One notes that these poverty rates are lower than those observed in the whole population, with the exception of Germany, Ireland and the UK. Without allowances, they are only lower in Nordic countries: Denmark, Finland and Sweden. This contrasts with what has been observed in the US, Canada or Australia (Atkinson *et al.* 1995). As to the efficiency scores, they are consistently higher for children than for the whole population, as expected. Those scores are particularly high in Belgium, France, Ireland, Luxembourg and the UK. They are low in the Scandinavian countries, Germany and the Netherlands. In fact, we have the same clustering as observed for the whole population, but the differences here are sharper.

Caution is needed in interpreting those numbers. First, as already seen, there are other ways of helping children: tax credits, maternity leave, housing subsidies, day care, which are not studied here. These other benefits, which are important in Scandinavian countries, explain why in these countries the rate of poverty of children is low even before introducing family allowances (*sensu stricto*). Secondly, efficiency depends on the generosity of the program; in other words one has to take into account the expenditure per child. In that respect, one can contrast Denmark with an efficiency score of 0.7 and generous family allowances with Ireland, that spends much less and yet exhibits an efficiency score of 3.7.

We thus decompose the efficiency score controlling for generosity in absolute terms or in relative terms. In either case, we use the lowest spender—Ireland or Germany depending on the approach chosen—as a yardstick. The efficiency score can now be divided into two parts: what is due to additional spending (naturally, this is zero for Ireland or Germany) and what is due to the benefit structure *per se*.

Table 13.6 provides two decompositions of the efficiency score for the whole population of each EU country. Clearly, we are interested by the conditional score which truly allows for a fair comparison of alternative benefit rules. There is not much difference between the two decompositions, except for countries such as Luxembourg, Germany or Denmark which do not rank the same way in absolute or in relative terms. Family allowances controlled for revenue size seem to be particularly efficient in Ireland and in Belgium. They have little effect in Sweden and in the other Scandinavian countries. Turning to the case of poverty among children, Table 13.7 gives much higher conditional scores with again the exception of Sweden.

Even if we control for generosity, the reduction in poverty can result from two factors: the benefit rule and the relation between family size and poverty.

Table 13.6. Decomposition of efficiency scores: overall poverty (LIS)

Country		Using the Irish envelope		Using the German share	
	Efficiency score	Conditional score	Revenue effect	Conditional score	Revenue effect
Belgium	3.0	1.4	1.6	1.7	1.3
Denmark	0.7	0.3	0.4	0.5	0.2
Finland	0.9	0.45	0.45	0.6	0.3
France	2.2	0.8	1.4	0.9	1.3
Germany	0.9	0.4	0.5	0.9	0.0
Ireland	3.7	3.7	0.0	3.0	0.7
Luxembourg	2.2	0.65	1.55	1.3	0.9
Netherlands	0.9	0.4	0.5	0.5	0.4
Sweden	0.3	0.1	0.2	0.2	0.1
UK	2.0	1.2	0.8	1.1	0.9

Table 13.7. Decomposition of efficiency scores: poverty among children (LIS)

Country	Efficiency score	Using the Irish envelope		Using the German share	
		Conditional score	Revenue effect	Conditional score	Revenue effect
Belgium	11.2	5.1	6.1	6.3	4.9
Denmark	3.1	1.7	1.4	2.4	0.7
Finland	3.6	2.0	1.6	2.6	1.0
France	10.1	3.6	6.5	4.2	5.9
Germany	4.1	2.5	1.6	4.1	0.0
Ireland	9.7	9.7	0.0	8.5	1.2
Luxembourg	9.0	3.0	6.0	5.5	3.5
Netherlands	3.7	1.6	2.1	2.3	1.4
Sweden	1.9	0.9	1.0	1.5	0.4
UK	8.6	4.5	4.1	3.8	4.8

Indeed, the benefit rule can vary across countries for good and bad reasons. A bad reason, at least as far as redistribution is concerned, is a policy exclusively aimed at fostering fertility. Typical of that is the benefit rule which would give allowances only to families with more than two children. The good reason would be to favor a given family type because it tends to be more likely to be poor. Suppose, for example, that large families tend to be poorer than families with two or less children. Then it makes sense to adopt a benefit rule biased towards families with more than two children.

13.4 **Types of child care policies**

Child care policies are often viewed as the most efficient way to encourage both fertility and female employment. They usually take three forms: publicly-funded child care, replacement income for parents who temporarily quit their job in order to take care of their infant (parental leaves), and financial support to help parents deal with child expenses (family allowances and tax benefits). In a recent paper, de Henau *et al.* (2005) assess the relative generosity of child policies in the EU15 and they also evaluate to what extent these policies are what they call 'dual-earner-family-friendly.'

Their research is based on an in-depth collection and aggregation of data. Table 13.8 provides their final ranking of EU15 countries in the three fields of child policy, along with a combined index. It allows for some interesting comparisons. The Nordic countries are the most generous as regards child care. Considering that their generosity scores regarding parental leave and above all cash and tax benefits are rather low, we can conclude that they have clearly chosen to support working families with children by focusing on public child

Table 13.8. Synthetic indicators of childcare policies

Index of childcare 0–6		Index of parental leaves		Index of cash and tax benefits		Combined index of the three fields (UN)	
DK	91.06	FR	80.84	LUX	80.3	DK	63.00
SE	69.09	FI	78.10	AT	67.1	SE	57.43
FI	46.34	PT	73.87	BE	64.0	LUX	53.65
FR	45.50	NL	70.96	GE	50.6	FR	52.11
IT	37.56	AT	66.53	IE	47.6	FI	51.20
BE	36.94	SE	63.73	EL	47.2	AT	50.09
LUX	36.67	ES	61.09	UK	43.3	BE	46.93
AT	33.38	LUX	60.95	FR	36.6	GE	40.15
GE	30.01	IT	56.93	FI	34.0	IT	40.11
NL	27.97	GE	49.93	NL	30.3	NL	39.29
UK	24.31	BE	49.78	IT	28.4	PT	35.91
PT	22.13	DK	43.87	SE	27.8	ES	27.66
ES	16.39	IE	31.17	DK	26.0	UK	27.16
EL	14.03	UK	16.67	PT	25.5	IE	23.11
IE	6.84	EL	12.72	ES	16.8	EL	21.99

Key to read the table: Scale from zero (worst performer on all variables) to 100 (best performer)
Source: de Henau *et al.* (2005)

care systems. When looking at the combined index, one finds these Nordic countries ranked well (1, 2 and 5).

At the other extreme, in the bottom ranks of the combined index, one finds the Southern countries (Portugal, Spain and Greece) and the two Anglo-Saxon countries. These also are the 'usual suspects.' Italy can be distinguished from the other countries of the South of Europe, particularly as regards child care programs. France and Belgium are ranked in the top. France leads for its generosity towards parental leave, but surprisingly is not well ranked for cash and tax benefits. The reason is that France grants no cash benefits for the first child in the family.

These numbers show sharp differences in the level and in the type of generosity of EU15 policies and these differences reflect the complexity of the issue. The policies pursue different objectives: poverty alleviation, horizontal equity, female employment and fertility. Regarding the latter, the conventional wisdom is that public child care facilities are a more efficient tool than family allowances.

13.5 **Conclusion**

In this chapter we have studied the effect of family allowances on poverty in a number of European countries. The first conclusion is that their effect is quite remarkable in some countries, particularly when focusing on poverty among children.

The second conclusion is that a large part of this effect is merely due to the amount of money that is spent. At the same time, we observe that after controlling for spending, alternative benefit rules applied to the same income distribution yield about the same scores. This implies that what really matters are not the differences in benefit rules, but the differences in the relative position of families with children with respect to the poverty line. In other words, family allowances are particularly efficient in countries where a number of families have their income slightly below the poverty level. As to the benefit rule *per se* it has a different incidence when it does treat all children equally, and family patterns vary.

14 Conclusion

14.1 Lionel or Tony

Over the Spring of 1997, socialist prime ministers were elected in both France and the UK. Tony Blair succeeded Conservative governments that had ruled the UK for more than a decade. By contrast Lionel Jospin's election was less of a rupture than that of Tony Blair's, since the socialists had been in power in France two years before.[1] Despite the common denomination of socialism, the difference between the two situations is tangible. For in the UK the Conservative governments of Margaret Thatcher first and of John Major later introduced drastic reforms into the British Welfare State. The power of the unions was broken and a number of social programs were abandoned, or tendered out to the private sector. As a result, one has the feeling that compared not only to France but to many other European countries, the UK is today quite different in its attitude towards entitlements, assistance and labor participation.

In the UK, a number of pressure groups with entrenched interests have lost ground. Entitlements have been restricted. The idea that income support ought to be limited in time is becoming prevalent. The perspective of welfare recipients has changed, particularly with regard to the vision of what recipients need to do for themselves, relative to what the state will do for them. More persistent job-search activities are in evidence. There is a wider acceptance of a labor market that generates high-variance wage and earnings distributions. In that respect, Tony Blair's 'New Contract for Welfare' was typical. It placed much of the responsibility for income support for families with low earnings capacity on their own efforts in the private labor market.

This apparent change in attitude and perspective is unthinkable in France. Since the start of the Fifth Republic, France has been ruled first by rightist governments, then by socialist governments. Right or left were equally conservative towards their social institutions and neither one has been able to modernize French society, particularly in terms of breaking their 'dependency' on public transfers and a number of privileges. In 1994, a rightist coalition came back to power when Prime Minister Juppé tried to reform some aspects of social

---

[1] Had the author been German speaking, he would have entitled this section 'Tony and Gerhard' (Schröder). To a large extent the French and the German welfare states face the same problem of entitlements and acquired rights. To illustrate this point, take the 35-hour-week introduced in France in 1999, and which is today under attack because it is boosting labor costs and doing little to create new jobs. The Germans do not have such a legal limit and yet it is a norm in Germany that has been negotiated by unions and employers.

protection by making it more sustainable and equitable. But he had to back down after several weeks of strikes for the vested interests were too powerful at blocking reforms.[2] Not surprisingly, most indicators show the French social protection system in urgent need of reform. But both the right and the left seem to agree on not taking the political risk of making it happen.

We do not want to suggest that everything is fine in the UK and bad in France. The UNDP indicator of welfare still puts France at the top of its ranking. We are merely conveying the idea often heard in the UK, that the Labour Party is grateful to the Conservatives for having done the dirty job for them, and that the French Socialist Party would have liked their political opponents to have done the same.

We firmly believe that most European countries need to go through a painful process of reform. And that basically amounts to breaking some vicious circles caused by entrenched interests, acquired rights, entitlements, persistent assistance. We believe that a drastic purge, such as the one experienced by the British, could be avoided, and that the same effects could be obtained more quietly. Yet, unfortunately, it is possible that some countries will be forced to 'lose weight' through a severe and harsh medical treatment, rather than through a progressive and reasonable diet.

14.2 **The acquired rights issue**

There is wide consensus that the main difficulty facing the welfare state is within itself. Clearly the issues of ageing, declining growth, globalization, family splits, increasing dependence and disincentives are real ones. But they can be solved with an appropriate reform of social protection. In other words, they can be solved if the welfare state can evolve and move away from sectors or people who are no longer in need.

Unfortunately, we live in a world where people feel entitled to benefits even when they have not contributed to them, and when they have enough resources to do without them. Examples of what is often called 'acquired rights' are numerous. To recap, these are rights which at one time were given to a category of people in order to meet particular and legitimate needs, but which have lost that legitimacy because those needs have disappeared, or have been eclipsed by other priorities. Such illegitimate entitlements might be, for example, rent control regulations when most of the beneficiaries are middle- and upper-middle class, pension regimes which involve benefits well above the young age earnings, agricultural policy that benefits well-to-do farmers.

---

[2] In 2002, another right-of-center Prime Minister, Jean-Pierre Raffarin, was elected with the intention of reforming the French Welfare State. It is facing many obstacles.

The removal of such entitlements is essential in order to bring fairness into the working of the welfare state, and above all, to provide it with additional resources. But caution is needed. Before assessing that an entitlement is illegitimate, one has to make sure that it is not the outcome of a commitment made behind the veil of ignorance to protect individuals against a reversal of fortune. What makes an entitlement illegitimate is that the law of probabilities, or the economic setting on which it was initially based, has changed significantly. Such changes could be an unexpected increase in longevity, a new medical technology, or an economic depression, which makes former commitments difficult or impossible to meet.

14.3 **Towards a European social protection**

We have observed a limited tendency towards convergence in spending levels, and in the broad structure of provision. Mediterranean countries with Social-Democratic governments have increased their level of spending, while at least some Northern governments have put a cap on it. There is also some narrowing down of the gap between Bismarckian and Beveridgean social insurance systems.

It is unclear how far this trend will go towards eroding the disparity between welfare and social insurance systems. As long as standards of living are different across European countries—and they should remain so for some time—it is not realistic to expect complete convergence in the near future. Some people advocate a voluntarist policy of harmonization, if not uniformization, of social protection systems. In so doing, they cannot expect low income countries to afford the same generous programs as the high income countries. Consequently, to be implemented, harmonizing social protection in the EU requires some important revenue sharing, but this is unlikely to be affordable, both politically and financially. This observation holds true even were the demand for harmonization to be cast in relative, rather than in absolute terms, that is to say, if social benefits vary across countries according to national median income.

It is clear that with increasing mobility, schemes providing benefits on the basis of work records are less exposed to erosion than schemes granting uniform or means-tested benefits. There is thus a case for organizing welfare programs at the European level that avoid an undeniable inflow of welfare recipients in the most generous countries, and ultimately a race to the bottom resulting in the death of welfare programs. Indeed, one likely outcome of economic integration and mobility, in the absence of supra-national intervention or international cooperation, is the generalization of Bismarckian systems, that is, systems that provide earnings-related benefits.

If national governments really come under pressure, particularly through the electoral process, to reduce that part of social spending that is essentially redistributive, there may arise a demand for a European safety net, that is, a minimum standard for social protection.

14.4 **Wrapping up**

It is now time to wrap up the main ideas of this book. We view the welfare state as an institution aimed at reducing poverty and providing protection to all. Yet the welfare state is not the only institution doing that. The market and the family can do it but with their own limitation: the market does not redistribute; the family lacks universality. The action of the welfare state is not restricted to one of spending; it operates also through laws and regulations that affect market and family decisions (minimum wage, parental duties). So far, the welfare state has been working quite well. It has reduced uncertainty and poverty. It has had positive effects on growth. At the same time the setting in which it now operates is different from what it was 50 years ago when initiated. Now it operates within a context of:

- family break-ups,
- tax competition and globalization,
- evolving labor markets.

The actors of the welfare state behave according to their own incentive structure, and that leads to productive and distributive inefficiencies. Funds are not always allocated to those who should benefit from them, and more and better services could be produced with fewer resources. All these factors, including new settings and inefficient behavior patterns, lead one to wonder whether the welfare state has not evolved like a dinosaur, increasingly ill adjusted to the surrounding world. Yet there is a difference: a world without dinosaurs happens to be quite livable. On the other hand without a welfare state, our society might well change for the worse. In any case, without going that far, these factors do put a heavy pressure on the welfare state, calling for reforms ranging from complete dismantlement to shallow plastic changes.

From the viewpoint of public economics, the reforms should include playing on the complementariness of the market and of the informal sector, changing the benefit rule so as to avoid costly Bismarckian schemes or means-tested programs. This viewpoint is sometimes perceived as naive or technocratic because it neglects the political dimension. More specifically, it is important to ensure political support to sustain a program, and to take into account political resistance from entrenched interests to any reform.

In theory, one can design a means-tested program that takes into account the problems raised by people who try to abuse the system on the grounds that the government cannot screen those who need assistance and those who do not. Yet in practise, because of a lack of political support, such a program will be progressively dismantled. In the final analysis, the poor will get less from it than from a program yielding uniform benefits to all.

In designing a viable program, it is crucial to incorporate those political constraints. It is just as important to be watchful so as not to end up with a program that is politically resistant, but does nothing or very little to help the needy. It is our view that there is always a cost in keeping social programs alive that don't effectively fulfill their basic objectives. Indeed, if the private sector does as well; these social programs had better be dropped.

Another equally important consideration is that of implications for the future. When designing a program, with the understanding that some of its benefits go to the non-needy, one has to control for the possibility of demographic or social changes that enable vested interests to divert the program from its original purpose. The reform of the welfare state is not an easy task. It consists of delicate choices. The first concern is the adding of non-needy beneficiaries for the purpose of ensuring political support, and not for their own sake. It is important to check that the program does not lose its impact because of it and does not do better than the private sector would.

The second delicate choice concerns commitment. It is essential that the welfare state be committed to fulfilling some tasks. Individuals want to count on social protection programs in the future, but at the same time they need to accept that some of them are contingent on demographic, economic or technological changes. In other words, 'yes' to commitment to principles but 'no' to specific spending. How can one reasonably promise a constant 75 per cent replacement ratio to retirees or full coverage of heart transplants in an evolving world? Fulfilling these promises can turn out to be socially inefficient because of other more pressing priorities.

Let us finally dare to make three recommendations. First, let us conduct a relentless fight against inefficiency. Secondly, let us retarget the priorities of the welfare state towards redistribution and poverty alleviation through programs offering uniform benefits to all. Access to supplementary schemes should be facilitated to allow reasonable replacement ratios to those who can afford them. Finally, let us avoid commitments that lead to unaffordable entitlements by making benefits contingent.

These reforms are urgent. Unfortunately, they do not look that way to the individual citizen. Nor do they look urgent to politicians who keep having a short run accounting view instead of a long run generational view of financial balances. Indeed, waiting for a crisis to force people to accept a long overdue reform is a mistake—not necessarily a deadly mistake, but at least a costly one. The welfare state is not a dinosaur, but it might become a Titanic. The icebergs are gleaming threateningly ahead. There is still time to avoid them.

BIBLIOGRAPHY

Aaberge, R., A. Bjrklund, M. Jantti, M. Palme, P. Pedersen, N. Smith and T. Wennemo, (2002). Income inequality and income mobility in the Scandinavian countries compared to the United States, *Review of Income and Wealth*, 48, 443–69.

Abott, M. and C. Doucouliagos, (2003). The efficiency of Australian universities: a data envelopment analysis, *Economics of Education Review*, 22, 89–97.

Adema, W., (1999). Net social expenditure, *Labor Market and Social Policy, Occasional Papers* n° 52, OECD, Paris.

Adema, W., (2001). Net social expenditure, second edition, *Labor Market and Social Policy, Occasional Papers* n° 39, OECD, Paris.

Adema, W., M. Einerhand, B. Eklind, J. Lotz and M. Pearson, (1996). Net public social expenditures, *Labor Market and Social Policy, Occasional Papers* n° 19, OECD, Paris.

Afonso, A., (2004). A note on public spending efficiency, *CESIfo-DICE Report, Journal of Institutional Comparisons*, 2, 35–9.

Afonso, A. and St. Aubyn, (2004). Non parametric approaches to education and health expenditures efficiency in the OECD countries, ISEG/UTL Department of Economics Working Paper.

Afonso, A., L. Schuknekt and V. Tanzi, (2003). Public sector efficiency: an international comparison, ECB Working Paper n° 24.

Agenor P-R., (2002). Does globalization hurt the poor? *Policy Research Working Paper 2922*, The World Bank.

Alesina, A. and G. M. Angeletos, (2002). Fairness and redistribution: US versus Europe, Harvard University, mimeo.

Alesina, A., E. Glaeser and B. Sacerdote, (2001). Why doesn't the US have a European type welfare state?, *Brooking Papers on Economic Activity*, Issue 2, 187–277.

Arnott, R. and J. Stiglitz, (1991). Moral hazard and non-market institutions: dysfunctional crowding out or pure monitoring?, *American Economic Review*, 81, 179–90.

Atkinson, A. B., (1991). Social insurance, *The Geneva Papers on Risk and Insurance Theory*, 16, 113–32.

Atkinson A. B., (1995). The welfare state and economic performance, *National Tax Journal*, vol. 48, 171–98.

Atkinson, A. B., (1996). *Incomes and the Welfare State*, Cambridge University Press, Cambridge.

Atkinson, A. B., (2000). *The Economic Consequences of Rolling Back the Welfare-State*, MIT Press, Cambridge, MA.

Atkinson, A. B., (2002). Income inequality in OECD countries: data and explanations, *CESifo Working Papers* n° 881.

Atkinson, A. B., L. Rainwater and T. M. Smeeding, (1995). *Income Distribution in OECD Countries*, OECD Policy Studies, OECD, Paris.

Banker, R. D., S. Janakiraman and R. Natarajan, (2004). Analysis of trends in technical and allocative efficiency: an application to Texas public school districts, *European Journal of Operational Research*, 154, 477–91.

Barr, N., (1992). Economic theory and the welfare state: a survey and interpretations, *Journal of Economic Literature*, 30, 741–803.

Barr, N., (1998). *The Economics of the Welfare State* (3rd edn), London: Oxford University Press.

Becker, G. S., (1991). *A Treatise on the Family*, (Enlarged Edition), Harvard University Press, Cambridge.

Beckerman, W. and S. Clark, (1982). *Poverty and Social Security in Britain since 1961*, Oxford University Press, Oxford.

Belan, P. and P. Pestieau, (1999). Privatizing social security: a critical assessment, *The Geneva Papers on Risk and Insurance. Issues and Practice*, 24, 114–30.

Beland, O., (2005). Insecurity, citizenship and globalization. The multiple faces of state protection, *Sociological Theory*, 23, 25–41.

Benabou, R. and J. Tirole, (2002). Beliefs in a just world and redistributive politics, Princeton University, mimeo.

Besley, T. and M. Gouveia, (1994). Health care, *Economic Policy*, 19, 200–58.

Beveridge, W. H., (1942). Social Insurance and Allied Services, Cmd 6404, London, HMSO.

Bisin, A. and T. Verdier, (2004). Work ethic and redistribution: a cultural transmission model of the welfare state, NYU and Delta, mimeo.

Bjrklund, A., T. Eriksson, M. Jantti, O. Raaum and E. Sterbacka, (2002). Brother correlations in earnings in Denmark, Finland, Norway and Sweden compared to the United States, *Journal of Population Economics*, 15, 757–72.

Bjurek, H., U. Kjulinet and B. Gustafson, (1992). Efficiency productivity and determinants of inefficiency at public care centers in Sweden, Working Paper, University of Gothenburg.

Blanchard, O. and J. Tirole, (2004). The optimal design of unemployment insurance and employment protection, NBER Working Paper.

Blondal, S. and S. Scarpetta, (1998). Falling participation rates among older workers in the OECD countries, Paris, OECD.

Boadway, R. and M. Marchand, (1995). The use of public expenditures for redistribution purpose, *Oxford Economic Papers*, 47, 45–59.

Boadway, R., M. Marchand, M. Leite Monteiro and P. Pestieau, (2003). Social insurance and redistribution, in S. Cnossen (ed.), *Public Finance and Public Policy in the New Millenium*, McMillan, 333–58.

Boldrin, M., J-J. Dolado, J-F. Gimeno and F. Perrachi, (1999). The future of pensions in Europe, *Economic Policy*, 29, 287–320.

Bosmans, N. and F. Fecher, (1998). Performance of Belgian hospitals: a frontier approach, *Health Economics*, 7, 263–77.

Boveroux, Ph., F. Debrule and H-J. Gathon, (1995). Efficiency and institutional arrangements in the Belgian nursing home industry, *Cahiers de Recherche du CREPP* n° 95–07.

Breen, R. and P. Moisis, (2003). Poverty dynamics for measurement error, ISER Working Papers, 2003–17.

Brown Ph. and R. Crompton (eds), (1994). *A New Europe? Economic Restructuring and Social Exclusion*, UCL Press, London.

Burgess, J-F. and P. W. Wilson, (1993). Decomposing hospital productivity changes 1985–1988: a non-parametric Malmquist approach, mimeo.

Burkhauser, R. V. and J. G. Poupore, (1997). A cross- national comparison of permanent inequality in the United States and Germany, *Review of Economic and Statistics*, 79, 10–17.

Burkhauser, R. V., D. Holtz-Eakin and S. E. Rhody, (1997). Mobility and inequality in the 1980s: a cross-national comparison of the United States and Germany, in *The Distribution of Welfare and Households Production*, S. P. Jenkins, A. Kapteyn and B. van Praag (eds), Cambridge University Press, Cambridge, MA, 111–75.

Burniaux, J-M., T. T. Dang, D. Fore, M. Förster, M. Mira d'Ercole and H. Hoxley, (1998). Income distribution and poverty in selected OECD countries, OECD Economics Department Working Paper #183, Paris.

Burniaux, J-M., R. Duval and F. Jaumotte, (2004). Coping with Ageing: a Dynamic approach to Quantify the Impact of Alternative Policy Options on Future Labour Supply in OECD Countries, Economic Department Working Paper, 371, OECD, Paris.

Cantillon, B. and K. van den Bosch, (2002). Back to the basics: the case for an adequate minimum guaranteed income in the active welfare state, in J. Pacolet and E. Claessens (eds), *Trade, Competitiveness and Social Protection*, AFP Press, 73–94.

Castel, R., (2003). The roads to disaffiliation: insecure work and vulnerable relationships, *International Journal of Urban and Regional Research*, 29, 519–35.

Castells, M., (2000). Material for an exploratory theory of the network society, *British Journal of Sociology*, 51, 5–24.

Cremer, H. and F. Gahvari, (1997). In-kind transfers, self-selection and optimal tax policy, *European Economic Review*, 41, 97–114.

Cremer, H. and P. Pestieau, (1996). Redistributive taxation and social insurance, *International Taxation and Public Finance*, 3, 259–80.

Cremer, H. and P. Pestieau, (2000). Reforming our pension systems: is it a demographic, financial or political problem?, *European Economic Review*, 44, 974–83.

Cremer, H. and P. Pestieau, (2004). Factor mobility and redistribution, Handbook in Urban Economics III, V. Smith and J. Thisse (eds), North Holland, Amsterdam, 2529–61.

Cremer, H., V. Fourgeaud, M. Leite-Monteiro, M. Marchand and P. Pestieau, (1997). Mobility and redistribution. A survey of the literature, *Public Finance*, 51, 325–52.

De Graeve, D. and T. Van Ourti, (2003). The Distributional Impact of Health Financing in Europe: A Review, in *The World Economy*, 23, 1459–79, Blackwell, London.

de Henau, J., D. Meulders and S. O'Dorchai, (2005). The childcare triad? Indicators assessing three fields towards dual-earner families in the EU15, unpublished, ULB, Brussels.

De Lathouwer, L., (2004). Reforming the passive welfare state: Belgium's new income arrangements to make work pay in internatonal perspectives, in P. Sounders (ed.), *Social Security and the Welfare to Work Transition*, vol. 10, International Studies on Social Security, Aldershot, Ashgate.

Deleeck, H., (1979). L'effet Matthieu, *Droit Social*, 11, 375–84.

Delhausse, B., S. Perelman and P. Pestieau, (1993). The distributive effects of shifting from public to private provision of retirement income, in J. Berghman and B. Cantillon (eds), *The European Face of Social Security*, Averbury, London, 145–56.

Dervaux, B., S. Jacobozone and H. Leleu, (1994). Productive and economic efficiency in French hospitals, mimeo.

Diamond, P., (1992). Organizing the health insurance market, *Econometrica*, 60, 1233–54.

Disney, R., (2004). Are contributions to public pension programmes a tax on employment?, *Economic Policy*, 19, 267–311.

EC, (1996). Tableaux de bord. Prélèvements obligatoires, European Commission, DGXXI, mimeo.

Erlandsen, E. and Forsund, F. R., (2002). Efficiency in the provision of municipal nursing and home care services: the Norwegian experience, in *Efficiency in the Public Sector*, Kevin Fox (ed.), Kluwer Academia Publishers, Amsterdam.

Esping-Andersen, G., (1990). *The Three Worlds of Welfare Capitalism*, Princeton University Press, Princeton.

Eurostat, (2005). Population and Social Conditions Statistics, <www.europa.eu.int>.

Eurostat, (2004). Structural Indicators of Social Cohesion, <www.europa.eu.int>.

Eurostat, (2003). European Social Statistics. Social Protection Expenditures and Receipts, 1991–2000, Luxembourg.

Ewald, F., (1986). *L'Etat-Providence*, Grasset, Paris.

Fenge, R. and P. Pestieau, (2005). *Social Security and Retirement*, MIT Press, Cambridge.

Ferrera, M., (1993). EC Citizens and Social Protection. Main results from an Eurobarometer survey, CEC, Div.V/E/2, Brussels.

Fields, G. S. and O. S. Mitchell, (1993). Reforming social security and social safety notes program in developing countries in *Developing Issues, Development Committee*, Washington, D.C., 32, 113–19.

Förster, F. M., (2003). Income inequalities, poverty and effects of social transfer policies in traditional OECD countries and Central Eastern Europe: patterns, trends and driving forces in the 1990s, Doctoral Thesis, University of Liège.

Förster, F. M. and M. Pearson, (2002). Income distribution and poverty in the OECD area: trends and driving forces, *OECD Economic Studies*, n° 34, Paris.

Gathon, H-J. and P. Pestieau, (1996). État providence et efficacité économique, *Revue Française d'Economie*, 11, 29–44.

Gill, I. S., T. T. Packard and J. Yermo, (2004). *Keeping the Promise of Social Security in Latin America*, The World Bank, Stanford University Press, Washington DC.

Gouyette, C. and P. Pestieau, (1999). Efficiency of the welfare state, *Kyklos*, 52, 537–53.

Grosskopf, S., D. Margaritas and V. Valdmanis, (2001). Comparing teaching and non-teaching hospitals: a frontier approach, *Health Care Management Science*, 4, 83–90.

Grosskopf, S., K. Hayes, L. Taylor and W. Weber, (1997). Budget-Constrained Frontier Measures of Fiscal Equality and Efficiency in Schooling, *Review of Economics and Statistics*, 79:1, 116–24.

Grubb, D. and W. Webb, (1993). Employment regulation and types of jobs in the European Community, *OECD Economic Studies*, 21, 7–62.

Gruber, J. and D. Wise (1999). Introduction and summary in *Social Security and Tax on Work around the World*, NBER, Chicago University Press, Chicago.

Gwartney, J. and R. Lawson (2001). Economic Freedom of the World, Annual Report, Cato Institute, Washington DC.

Hassler, J., J. Rodriguez Mora, K. Storesletten and F. Zilibotti, (2003). The survival of the welfare state, *American Economic Review*, 93, 87–112.

Haveman, R., (1997). The welfare state and full employment, in *Beyond 2000*, OECD, Paris.

Herbertson, T. and J. M. Orszag, (2003). The early retirement burden assuming the cost of the continued prevalence of early retirement in OECD countries, IZA Discussion Paper n° 816.

Holvad, T. and J.-L. Hougaard, (1993). Measuring technical input efficiency for similar production units: 80 Danish hospitals, European University Institute, Working Paper n° 93/36.

Illich, I., (1997). *Limits to Medicine. The Medical Nemesis. The Expropriation of Health*, Harmondsworth, NY.

Kaldor, N., (1956). Alternative theories of distribution, *Review of Economic Studies*, 23, 83–100.

Kooreman, P., (1994). Nursing home care in The Netherlands: a nonparametric efficiency analysis, *Journal of Health Economics*, 13, 301–16.

Kooreman, P., (1995). Data envelopment analysis and parametric frontier estimation: complementary tools, *Journal of Health Economics*, 13, 345–6.

Korpi, W. and J. Palma, (2003). New politics and class politics in the context of austerity and globalization: welfare states regress in 18 countries, 1975–95, *American Political Science Review*, 97, 425–46.

Kotlikoff, L. J. and A. Spivak, (1981). The Family as an incomplete annuities market, *Journal of Political Economy*, 89, 372–91.

Krugman, P. (1995). Growing World trade: causes and consequences, *Brookings Papers on Economic Activity*, 1, 327–62.

Krugman, P., (1996). The causes of high unemployment. The inequality or unemployment trade-off, *Policy Options*, 17, n° 6, 20–4.

Kunreuther, H., (1978). *Disaster Insurance Protection. Public Policy Lessons*, John Wiley, New York.

Kuznets, S., (1955). Economic growth and income inequality, *American Economic Review*, 45, 1–28.

Le Grand, J., (1982). *The Strategy of Equality Redistribution and the Social Services*, George Allen & Unwin, London.

Leonard, H. B. and R. J. Zeckhauser, (1983). Public insurance provision and non-market failures, *The Geneva Papers*, 8, 147–57.

Lindbeck, A., (1995a), Welfare states disincentives with endogenous habits and norms, *Scandinavian Journal of Economics*, 97, 477–94.

Lindbeck, A., (1995b), Hazardous welfare-state dynamics, *American Economic Review*, 85, Papers and Proceedings, 9–15.

Lindbeck, A., S. Nyberg and J. Weibull, (1999). Social norms and economic incentives in the welfare state, *Quarterly Journal of Economics*, 114, 1–35.

Lindert, P., (2004). *Growing Public: Social Spending and Economic Growth since the Eighteenth Century*, Cambridge University Press, Cambridge.

LIS, (2000). Luxembourg Income Study Key Figures, <www.lisproject.org>.

Mancebón, M. and E. Bandrés, (1999). Efficiency evaluation in secondary schools: the key role of model specification and *ex post* analysis of results, *Education Economics*, 7:2, 131–52.

Maddison, A., (1991). *Dynamic Forces in Capitalist Development*, Oxford University Press, Oxford.

Marchand, M. and P. Pestieau, (1996). L'état ou le marché dans l'assurance maladie, *Revue Française d'Economie*, 11, 3–20.

Marx, I. and G. Verbist, (1997). Low- wage employment and poverty: curse or cure? An explorative study using the LIS datasets, mimeo.

Masson, A., (2003). Économie des solidarités, *Les Solidarités Familiales en Question*, D. Debordeaux and P. Strobel, Librairie Générale de Droit et de Jurisprudence, Paris, 143–214.

Masson, A., (2004). Les pouvoirs publics et la famille, *Cahiers Français*, 322, 81–7.

Meister, W. and W. Ochel, (2003). Tax privileges for families in an international comparison, *CESifo Dice Report*, 1, 42–5.

Meyers, M., (2004). A devolution revolution? Change and continuity in US state social policies in the 1990s, Eleventh International Research Seminar on Issues in Social Security, Sigtuna, Sweden.

Mitchell, O., (1997). Administrative costs in public and private retirement systems, in *Privatizing Social Security*, M. Feldstein (ed.), Chicago University Press, Chicago.

Morrison, P. C., (2002). Productive structure and efficiency of public hospitals, in *Efficiency in the Public Sector*, Kevin Fox (ed.), Kluwer Academia Publishers, Amsterdam.

Ng, Ying Chu and Spng Ko Li, (2000). Measuring the research performance of Chinese higher education institutions: an application of data envelopment analysis, 8:2, 139–56.

Nolan, B. and I. Marx, (2000). Low pay and household poverty, in G. Salverda and S. Bazen, *Laborer Market Inequalities: Problems and Policies in International Perspective*, Oxford, Oxford University Press.

OECD, (1996a), Earnings inequality, low paid unemployment and earnings mobility, in *Employment Outlook*, OECD, Paris, 59–99.

OECD, (1996b), Ageing in OECD countries. A Critical Policy Challenge, *Social Policy Studies* n° 26.

OECD, (2000a), *Reform for an Ageing Society*, Social Issues, OECD, Paris.

OECD, (2000b), OECD Employment Outlook 2000, OECD, Paris.

OECD, (2001a), OECD Social Expenditure Database, 1980–98, OECD, Paris.

OECD, (2001b), OECD Employment Outlook 2001, OECD, Paris.

OECD (2004a), Social Expenditure Database (SOCX, www.oecd.org/els/social/expenditure).

OECD, (2004b), Annual National Accounts of OECD members countries, vol. 1, Paris.

OECD, (2004c), OECD Health Data 2004: a comparative analysis of 30 countries, OECD, Paris.

OECD (2004d), OECD Employment Outlook 2004, OECD, Paris.

OECD (2004e), Labor Market Statistics, OECD Website, OECD, Paris.

OECD, (2005). Income distribution and poverty in OECD countries in the second half of the 1990s, unpublished.

Okun, A. M., (1974). *Equality and Efficiency*, Washington, The Brookings Institution.

Ooghe, E., E. Schokkaert and J. Fléchet, (2003). The incidence of social security contributions: an empirical analysis, *Empirica*, 30.

Osterkamp, R., (2004). Measuring efficiency of health-care provision: intercountry comparison and changes over time, unpublished.

Persson, T. and G. Tabellini, (1994). Is inequality harmful for growth?, *American Economic Review*, 84, 600–21.

Pestieau, P., (1994). Social protection and private insurance. Reassessing the role of public versus private sector in insurance, *The Geneva Papers on Risk and Insurance Theory*, 19, 81–92.

Pestieau, P., (2003a), Raising the age of retirement to ensure a better retirement, *Geneva Papers on Risk and Insurance. Issues and Practice*, 28, 686–95.

Pestieau, P., (2003b), Aging, retirement and pension reforms, *The World Economy*, 26, 1447–57.

Pestieau, P., (2004). Globalization and redistribution, unpublished.

Pestieau, P. and H. Tulkens, (1993). Assessing and explaining the performance of public sector activities, *FinanzArchiv*, 50, 293–323.

Petrella, R., (1995). *Limits to Competition*, MIT Press, Cambridge, Mass.

Pierson, P., (1997). *Dismantling the Welfare State? Reagan, Thatcher and the Politics of Retrenchment*, Cambridge University Press, Cambridge, Mass.

Pierson, P., (2001). Coping with permanent austerity: welfare state restructuring in affluent democracies, in P. Pierson (ed.), *The New Politics of the Welfare State*, Oxford University Press, Oxford.

Poterba, J., (1996). Government intervention in the markets for education and healthcare: how and why?, in V. Fuchs (ed.), *Individual and Social Responsibility*, Chicago University Press, Chicago, 277–304.

Purton, H., (1996). European welfare state in the 1990s. An economic analysis of the challenge and efforts at reform, Research Report n° 19, CEPS, Brussels.

Ravallion, M., (2001). On assessing the efficiency of the Welfare State: A comment, *Kyklos*, 54, 115–24.

Ravallion, M., (2003). The debate on globalization, poverty and inequality: why measurement matters, *International Affairs*, 79, 739–53.

Razin, A. and E. Sadka, (2005). The Decline of the Welfare State: Demographics and Globalization, MIT Press, Cambridge, MA.

Rochet, J-Ch., (1991). Incentives, redistribution and social insurance, *The Geneva Papers on Risk and Insurance Theory*, 16, 143–66.

Rosenvallon, P., (1995). *La Nouvelle Question Sociale*, Seuil, Paris.

Salinas, J., F. Pedraja-Chaparro and P. Smith, (2004). Evaluating the introduction of a quasi-maker in community care: a Malmquist index approach, *Socio Economic Planning Science*, 37, 1–13.

Sandmo, A., (1991). Economists and the welfare state, *European Economic Review*, 35, 213–39.

Sandmo, A., (1995). Introduction. The welfare economics of the welfare state, *Scandinavian Journal of Economics*, 97, 469–76.

Sexton, T. R., A. M. Leiken, S. Sleeper and A. F. Coburn, (1989). The impact of prospective reimbursement on nursing home efficiency, *Medical Care*, 27, 154–63.

Sinn H-W., (1990). Tax harmonization and tax competition in Europe, *European Economic Review*, 34, 489–504.

Sinn, H-W., (1995). A theory of the welfare state, *Scandinavian Journal of Economics*, 97, 495–26.

Sneessens, H., F. Shadman and O. Pierrard, (2003). Effets des préretraites sur l'emploi, Actes du 15e Congrès des Economistes belges de Langue française, CIFoP, Charleroi.

Snower, D. J., (1994). The future of the welfare state, *CEPR Occasional Paper*, n° 13.

Solow, R. M., (1998). *Work and Welfare*, Princeton University, Princeton, N.J.

Sorensen, P. B., (2000). The case for international tax co-ordination reconsidered, *Economic Policy*, 31, 429–72.

Stigler, G., (1965). The tenable range of functions of local government, in E. Phelps (eds), *Private Wants and Public Needs*, Norton, New York City, 167–76.

Stiglitz, J., (1983a), Risk, incentive and insurance, *The Geneva Papers*, 8, 4–33.

Stiglitz, J., (1983b), On the social insurance. Comments on 'The State and the demand for security in contemporary societies', *The Geneva Papers*, 8, 105–10.

Storms, B., (1995). L'effet Matthieu dans le domaine de l'accueil des enfants, Centrum voor Social Beleid, UFSIA, Antwerpen.

Strengmann-Kuhn, W., (2002). Working poor in Europe: a partial basic income for workers?, unpublished.

Svallfors, S., (1997). World of welfare and attitudes to redistribution: a comparison of eight Western nations, *European Sociological Review*, 13, 283–304.

Summers, L., J. Gruber and R. Vergara, (1993). Taxation and the structure of labor markets: the case of corporatism, *Quarterly Journal of Economics*, 107, 385–411.

Townsend, P., (1979). *Poverty in the United Kingdom*, Penguin Harmondsworth, London.

UN (2001). United Nations World Population prospects: the 2000 revisions, N.Y.

UN (1998). United Nations World Population prospects, N.Y.

Valdes-Prieto, S., (1998). Administrative costs in a privatized pension system. Paper presented at the Pensions Systems Reform in Central America Conference, Cambridge, Mass.

Van Doorslaer, E. K. A., H. Bleichrodt, S. Calonge, U-G. Gerdtham, M. Gerfin, J. Geurts, L. Gross, U. Hakkinen, R. E. Leu and A. Wagstaff, (1997). Income related inequalities in health: some international comparisons, *Journal of Health Economics*, 16, 93–112.

Vandenbroucke, F., (2001). The active welfare state: a social democratic ambition for Europe, *The Policy Network Journal*, 1.

Varian, H., (1980). Redistributive taxation as social insurance, *Journal of Public Economics*, 14, 46–68.

Whelan, Ch., R. Layte and B. Maitre, (2003). Persistent income poverty and depreciation in the European Union. An analysis of the first three waves of the European Community Household Panel, *International Social Policy*, 32, 1–18.

Wildasin, D., (1995). Factor mobility, risk and redistribution in the welfare state, *Scandinavian Journal of Economics*, 97, 527–46.

World Bank, (1999). *Averting the Old Age Crisis*, Oxford University Press, Oxford.

Wyckoff, J. H. and J. Lavigne, (1991). The technical inefficiency of public elementary schools in New York, Working Paper SUNY Albany, N.Y.

GLOSSARY

Active welfare state Social policy aiming for an active and responsible society while maintaining the objective of adequate social protection. The objective is a stronger integration between social, fiscal and employment policies.

Actuarial principle Applied to social protection finance, it means that the contribution (premium) is determined by the size of the expected benefit to be received.

Adverse selection The situation that occurs when the people most likely to receive benefits from a certain type of insurance are the most likely ones to purchase it. The problem can be overcome by making insurance mandatory if possible. And if not, by policies targeted toward specific risk groups.

Altruism Concern for the well-being of others, as opposed to self-interest.

Annuity A payment that lasts until recipient's death.

Best practise frontier The curve showing the maximum amount of production that can be achieved with given resources. It is constructed on the basis of a sample of production units.

Capitation-based reimbursement A system in which medical care is provided for a set of individuals for a fixed monthly fee.

Categorical benefits These benefits are provided to individuals who belong to a specific category, or who meet specific eligibility criteria.

Child care Care provided for children by someone other than the parents of those children.

Co-insurance rate The proportion of costs above the deductible for which an insured individual is liable.

Cost-based reimbursement A system in which health care providers report their costs to the government and receive payment in that amount.

Commitment The capacity of policymakers to announce policy in advance and to stick to it regardless of changes in the economic environment, or in individual expectations.

Constitutional approach A two-stage collective decision process. In the first stage the 'rules of game', namely the constitution, are chosen behind the veil of ignorance, so to speak. In the second stage decisions are made through the political process.

Consumer's surplus It refers to the area under an individual's demand curve that measures the benefit derived from buying a commodity at a particular price.

Deadweight-loss Also called excess-burden, it refers to the loss in revenue brought about by a distortionary tax relative to a lump-sum tax for the same reduction in utility.

Decommodification Applied to social protection, it means that benefits and services provided by the welfare state are given as a right, not in exchange for past contributions.

Defined benefit A provision of a pension scheme by which the benefits to be received by the pensioner do not depend on the financial performance of the pension scheme.

Defined contribution A provision of a pension scheme by which the rules fix the contributions to the scheme; the benefit depends on the contribution plus the investment return.

Dependency ratio The ratio of people aged 65+ over those aged between 20 and 64.

Distortionary tax A tax that affects the individual's economic behavior and causes a deadweight loss.

Dual labor market Market with two classes of workers those with permanent contracts (insiders) and those with temporary contracts (outsiders).

Early retirement age Earliest age at which a public pension recipient can receive reduced benefits.

Earning income tax credit The EITC is essentially a subsidy to the earnings of low-income families which enables the working poor to escape poverty while it improves their work incentives. However, because of the need to phase out this subsidy when earnings are high enough, the EITC creates disincentives to work for people in the phase-out range.

Earnings-related benefits Applied to a social insurance program, this means that the amount of benefits or services is related to the level of contributions, themselves linked to earnings. (Also called Bismarckian.)

Effective retirement age The actual retirement age taking into account early retirement and special regimes.

Efficiency or Pareto efficiency An allocation of resources is (Pareto) efficient if no person can be made better off, without making some else worse off.

Efficiency wage The wage which employers accept to pay even if it is higher than the equilibrium wage because it reduces shirking and abstenteeism.

Entitlement principle A principle which holds that individuals are to be regarded as entitled to the rights of benefits or property so long as these are obtained by legitimate means. The adoption of such a principle can severely limit the capacity of government when the circumstances in which the rights were granted change 'unexpectedly.'

Entitlement programs Programs whose expenditures are determined by the number of people who qualify, rather than by preset budget allocations.

Equity Also called distributive equity, it implies an idea of fairness or justice regarding the manner in which the economy's resources are distributed among individuals.

Equity–efficiency trade-off The choice society must make between the total size of the economic pie and its distribution among individuals.

Equity premium paradox This refers to the long term historical regularity that the equity market has significantly outperformed the bond market, even after adjusting for risk.

Equivalence scale A weighting factor applied to the income of households of different sizes; it allows for a comparison of income that one calls adjusted or standardized income.

Experience rating Calculation of contributions based on the lay-off activity of the firm. More generally, making the price of an insurance a function of realized outcomes.

Family allowance The benefit paid to the parents (sometimes the mother) or guardian of dependent children. They are a universal benefit in contrast with the US AFDC (Aid to Families with Dependant Children) which is a means-tested program targeted to needier families.

Fiscalization A movement of social protection financing from (earmarked) payroll taxation to general taxation.

Flat rate benefits All who qualify receive the same amount of benefits or the same services, thus not related to earnings or contributions. (Also called universalistic or Beveridgean.)

Fully-funded scheme A scheme in which individuals contribute a portion of their salaries into a fund that accumulates interest over time. In retirement, pension benefits are financed by the principal and accrued interest.

Gini coefficient A measure of inequality that ranges from 0 to 1, and is equal to twice the area between the 45 degree line and Lorenz curve.

Health Maintenance Organization (HMO) Health care organization that integrates insurance and delivery of care by, for example, paying its own doctors and hospitals a salary independent of the amount of care they deliver.

Insiders and outsiders The distinction which helps to explain the persistence of unemployment. Unions and employers together determine the level of employment and wages of the insiders, generally the union members, at the expense of the outsiders whose wages and job security are lower.

Involuntary unemployment The unemployment which is not desired by the unemployed person (contrasted with voluntary unemployment).

Leaky bucket Metaphor introduced by Arthur Okun illustrating the loss of efficiency inherent in the redistribution process.

Lorenz curve A curve that shows the cumulative proportion of income that goes to each cumulative proportion of the population, starting with the lowest income group.

Lump-sum tax A tax that has no effect on the individual's behavior on, e.g., the labor or the capital market. Its amount is thus independent of a person's income, consumption of goods and services, or wealth. A typical lump-sum tax is the head or the poll tax.

Managed competition A system that bands people into large organizations that purchase insurance on their behalf.

Marginal tax rate The proportion of the last euro of income taxed by the government.

Market failure A situation that refers to the inability of market forces to attain efficiency. It generally arises because of externalities, market imperfections, asymmetric information, etc.

Matthew effect The perverse effect of redistributive programs that end up benefiting the non-needy, rather than the needy.

Means-tested benefits These benefits are paid to individuals only if income and wealth are below a certain level.

Merit good A good or a service the consumption of which is deemed to be intrinsically desirable, even though individuals are unwilling to purchase an adequate quantity of it.

Minimum wage It is a price floor meant to ensure that those who work earn enough to support a family. It is generally fixed above the full employment equilibrium wage, and it does create some unemployment.

Moral hazard When an individual's behavior is affected by the fact of being insured. It is *ex ante* if insurance increases the probability of the insured event; it is *ex post* if insurance increases the consumption of services following the occurrence of the insured event.

New social question This is the questioning of redistribution (through taxation or social insurance) decided behind the veil of ignorance. For one can increasingly foresee a wide range of individual risks: mortality, disease, unemployment, etc.

OMC (Open Method of Coordination) The process whereby common goals are laid down and progress is measured against jointly agreed indicators, while best practice is identified and compared.

Parental leave Compensation given to either mothers or fathers who temporarily quit their job to take care of their infant.

Pay-as-you-go A pension system under which benefits paid to current retirees come from payments made by current workers.

Payroll tax Also called social insurance contribution, it refers to a tax based on the wages and salaries paid by an employer and used to finance social insurance.

Political economy This is an approach to economics that focuses on the practical aspects of political action. It is a positive as opposed to a normative approach.

Poverty gap The relative amount of money required to raise the income of all poor households to the poverty line.

Poverty line A fixed level of income considered enough to provide a minimally adequate standard of living. A poverty line often used is half the median income.

Poverty rate The percentage of households with adjusted income below the poverty line.

Poverty trap The situation wherein a family loses from working: its earnings plus net transfers are inferior to net transfers when not working.

Prisoner's dilemma This term arises from the case of two arrested criminals who are subject to separate interrogations. Rationally, each should confess hoping that the other one will not do so. But as both will be motivated to act in their own perceived interest, they will both end up worse than if they had been able to agree between themselves not to confess. This model shows that rational behavior at the micro-level leads to an apparently irrational macro-outcome.

Productive inefficiency Also called efficiency slack, it occurs when the performance of a production unit lies below the efficiency (best practise) frontier.

QUALYS (quality adjusted life expectancy) This indicator gives the number of years left to an individual, e.g., after a surgical operation, but weighted to reflect the physical and psychological capacity that this individual might lose.

Race to the bottom If location decisions are influenced by the available tax–welfare package, national governments acting non-cooperatively are induced to adopt a less generous social policy than they would do in autarky.

Regression An analysis that involves the fitting of an (linear) equation to a set of data points for establishing quantitative economic relationships.

Regressive Used for a tax system under which an individual's average tax rate decreases with income.

Replacement rate The social insurance benefit an individual receives as a proportion of income earned when working.

Social dumping Imposing lower social contributions and taxes in export markets than are imposed in home markets, with the consequence that the generosity of social protection declines.

Self insurance This happens when an individual, instead of using an outside insurance device, relies on his own risk diversification or on his own wealth (saving for retirement).

Single provider A system that provides all citizens, regardless of income and health status, with a set of health care services at no direct cost to the insured.

Social security trust fund A fund in which social security payroll taxes that are not used for paying out benefits now are accumulated.

Social security wealth Also called pension rights, it is the present value of expected future social security benefits. When called *net* social wealth, the present value of future contributions is substracted.

Tax competition Imposing lower taxes on factors of production that could unfavorably move out of the country.

Tax expenditure A loss of tax revenue because some item is excluded from the tax base.

Tax shifting The difference between statutory incidence and economic incidence.

Third-party payment Payment for services by someone other than the provider or consumer.

Veil of ignorance This notion of 'being behind the veil of ignorance', or in the original position, refers to an imaginary situation in which people have no knowledge of their place in society.

Workfare Able-bodied individuals who qualify for welfare support receive it only if they agree to participate in a work-related activity.

Yardstick competition Applied to a federation or a confederation, it is the process whereby voters can exert their political sights by making meaningful comparisons between juridictions on the basis of their respective performance.

☐ INDEX

The letter f denotes a figure and t a table.